Retirement Rebel

Retirement Rebel

One woman, one motorhome,
one great big adventure

Siobhan Daniels

Vertebrate Publishing, Sheffield
www.adventurebooks.com

Retirement Rebel

*One woman, one motorhome,
one great big adventure*

Siobhan Daniels

First published in 2022 by Vertebrate Publishing.

 VERTEBRATE PUBLISHING
Omega Court, 352 Cemetery Road, Sheffield S11 8FT, United Kingdom.
www.adventurebooks.com

This book is a work of non-fiction based on the life of Siobhan Daniels. The author
has stated to the publishers that, except in such minor respects not affecting the
substantial accuracy of the work, the contents of the book are true.

A CIP catalogue record for this book is available from the British Library.

ISBN: 978-1-83981-179-1 (Paperback)
ISBN: 978-1-83981-180-7 (Ebook)

10 9 8 7 6 5 4 3 2 1

Edited by Moira Hunter.

Cover design by Jane Beagley, layout and production by Rosie Edwards, Vertebrate Publishing.
www.adventurebooks.com

Vertebrate Publishing is committed to printing on paper from sustainable sources.

Printed and bound in Great Britain by Clays Ltd., Elcograf S.p.A.

Contents

To

My daughter Samantha Hibbard-Daniels
for believing in my crazy dream.

Paddy and Lorraine Daniels for their never-ending support.

Maggie and Ann for their unwavering friendship.

Lucy at Flow yoga studio, Tunbridge Wells, for starting me
on my journey of self-belief and empowerment.

My little cuz Clare for always supporting my dreams.

Introduction

I ran into the toilet cubicle at work and locked the door behind me, sobbing uncontrollably, my body shaking. I felt totally distraught and angry. I looked at myself in the mirror and could see my raw emotions looking back at me, which made me sob even more. I had just been confronted about something, I don't even remember what now. For well over twenty years I had been working as a news presenter, reporter and producer in radio and television, and doing a very good job. I knew my job inside out and yet here I was, reduced to a blubbering mess hiding away in the ladies' toilets. For a long time now, in my fifties, I felt my work and my ability to do it had been undermined and questioned. It felt to me like everything I did was put under a microscope. I felt my age was against me in the workplace and stories were being given to far more junior and inexperienced staff.

My stress levels were so high I was unable to sleep. I would toss and turn in bed imagining conversations I would have with people I worked with, if I only had the courage. All that courage just dissipated as I got ready for work. I dreaded going into the office but would put on my makeup – my 'game face' – and head into work each day, even though in reality I felt totally broken.

In the latter years most days I would walk home from work sobbing after being berated in front of my colleagues, often for things that were out of my control. I was made to feel as if I was not a valued member of the team. Every day I felt upset about situations in the office and how I felt I was being treated. I would fight back tears because I didn't want to show how I truly felt, but deep in the pit of my stomach I felt sick. I would feel overwhelmed with panic and unable to recall information any more. My menopausal brain didn't help. I called it my 'cotton wool head'. I even forgot names of people I had worked with for years. I would look at them and in my head I was thinking, 'What's their name? I know I know their name. Why can't I remember it?' It was an awful feeling. It made me feel anxious at the best of times.

I felt there was no understanding at work of women who were going through the menopause. You couldn't have that difficult conversation to explain what was going on; how you were struggling, feeling exhausted due to lack of sleep because of hot flushes and your head full of all the stressful conversations at work, or worrying that you didn't have the same mental sharpness at the moment. You knew that your performance might not be up to par, so you would have loved to do a particular type of work until it settled. When I did try to tell them what impact the menopause was having on me and my work, it fell on deaf ears and my work performance was actually questioned, which only added to the stress.

It triggered something in me from my childhood and brought back all my childhood horrors. I am one of eight children, and my Irish father, Jimmy, who had multiple sclerosis, was very strict. He had been brought up by strict parents who would give him what he called 'a good hiding', and that was the way he was with us. For most of my childhood I remember him walking with a walking stick. I was very afraid of him because he would use that stick to beat us and we would be locked in the damp, dark cellar overnight as punishment. I am still very scared of dark, confined spaces to this day. He would shout at us and make us queue up outside the sitting room to wait our turn for a 'good hiding'. I would hear my siblings cry out as they were given their punishment and watch them emerge from the room looking traumatised and crying, and then it was my turn. I remember that fear I felt inside as a child. I would never be able to respond properly when he asked me a question because of that fear, and I knew my lack of response would warrant another 'good hiding'.

Now, even though I was in my fifties, some people I worked with could still make me feel like that lost, frightened little girl. That feeling of foreboding was palpable. When I felt I was mistreated at work, my brain would just clam up with fear.

I also missed the support of family at the time, but when I wanted to visit them in the north of England that too was often fraught with problems. I was made to feel my requests for certain rota shifts to allow me to travel were too difficult to accommodate. This compounded my sense of sadness and worthlessness in a job I had previously thrived in for over two decades.

As I was crying in the toilet cubicle I knew at that moment I could not carry on this way. No, not could not, *would* not. I had had enough. I was not prepared to put up with behaviour that made me feel so stressed and at times suicidal. I had to hatch an escape plan. I didn't know then what size or shape my plan would be, but I did know that I needed to do something drastic to cope with the things happening around me.

Feeling exhausted and increasingly marginalised and invisible at work, I had dragged myself into the office for the late shift. I was nervous about how I would actually get through the day as I struggled to cope with the raw drama I faced daily in my working life. I was losing who I was.

I had said to my daughter that morning that I was going into that black hole, where I had to just pretend to get through life ... that sometimes I didn't feel like pretending any more. And that scared me.

I eventually pulled myself together in the bathroom. I washed my face and reapplied my lipstick. Ignoring my bloodshot eyes, I told myself out loud, 'You can do this, you'll be okay', and I unlocked the door ... took a few deep breaths ... and went back into work. People were obviously aware that I had been upset, but we all tried to carry on as normal to get the job done.

I noticed on my phone that there were a couple of missed calls from my sister Helen, which was strange as she didn't often call me at work. I got a feeling of foreboding and wondered if there was something wrong with our mother, who was in her eighties and lived in Leeds. I made a mental note to call her during my break a little later on. For now I needed to concentrate on doing my job.

Most of the staff went home after the programme. There were just a few of us left to output the late news bulletin. I went to the top of the office to take my break and called my sister. She answered the phone very quickly. I said I was sorry I'd missed her calls earlier and asked if there was anything wrong. There was a long pause at the other end of the phone; then she explained to me that she had been diagnosed with lung cancer. I felt like I'd been punched in the stomach. I couldn't take in what she was telling me. Only four years earlier our brother Jonathan had died of lung cancer aged fifty-three. Now, at the same age, Helen was facing the same life-threatening illness. I could hardly breathe, but listened as she told me what the doctors had said. She was optimistic she could fight it and I tried to sound optimistic too. Inside my head I was screaming, 'Noooooooo, this cannot be true.' Helen was such a great big sister. She was the matriarch of the family, a pillar of strength for all of us in various ways as our mother aged. I just could not envisage life without her.

When I eventually got off the phone I crumbled. I was done. This was too much. It was just too awful to get my head around. I was consumed with anger. My sister could be dying and that was all that mattered to me now.

This was a crossroads in my life.

Only hours ago I was thinking about my dissatisfaction with my work situation, but all that just paled into insignificance now. I was being shown that life is precious and can be taken away so easily.

I could allow myself to be overwhelmed by all this, or I could use it to spur me on to dig deep, face my fears and find an alternative way of living; a positive way of ageing ... My escape plan had begun. I was going to fathom out a way to break free and live my life the way I wanted to, for as long as I had left, even if it took me a while to execute that plan. What was I going to do? How was I going to make it happen? I had a few years before I could retire and not much money. Despite that, I knew then that my life just had to change. But how?

Chapter 1

Bereavement

I woke up the next day and it hit me hard that my sister Helen had cancer. I was blindsided by her diagnosis. She started her chemotherapy treatment straight away and I was optimistic she would beat it. A couple of months later I caught the train up to Leeds to see her for lunch. It was then that I realised just how poorly she was. She had greeted me at the station in a taxi and we went to the Jamie Oliver restaurant. When she got out of the taxi I was pleased to see just how pretty and well she looked. She was wearing a beautiful long floaty, flowery dress. We waited for our table and chatted. When the waiter approached and said they had a table for us upstairs Helen looked scared and told them she wouldn't be able to climb the stairs. I knew then that she was far more poorly than I had realised. We had a long chat and I asked if she was afraid of dying; she said she wasn't. She was just heartbroken at having to leave her husband and children and she was trying to put things in order. That was the last time I saw my sister conscious. She died in the November, less than six months after being diagnosed.

I was heartbroken, devastated. I just could not deal with my grief. All my energy went into getting myself into work and surviving the shift. I would then retreat to my bed for days on end, with no real sense of purpose. When people asked me if I wanted to go out I made excuses because I was depressed. I knew I wasn't performing as well as I could at work. I was hanging on to everything by a thread. I put on a lot of weight and just cried for hours lying on the sofa.

My amazing daughter, Samantha, who since she was very young has been a voice of reason, struggled seeing me just slobbing on the sofa and crying all the time. I became a single mother when she was four, and she had seen me just getting on with life, facing difficulties as they came along and forging a career in radio and TV. Now I was retreating from life and not coping at all well. She encouraged me to go to the doctor, where I managed, through floods of tears, to explain how I was truly feeling at times: as if I didn't want to go on but at the same time I knew I had to for my daughter's sake. Finally I admitted that I needed help. The doctor was very understanding and made me realise I was going through a lot. She put me on anti-depressants. I also sought some counselling, which did help for a while.

I still had this feeling inside me that I needed to do something to regain my life. Retirement was not an option yet, but I knew I needed to change something and to at least get fit. I had to do something to push me out of my comfort zone and to believe in myself, especially when other people were talking down to me and making me feel worthless.

That was when my daughter had a brainwave. Arriving home one day and seeing me in my usual prone position on the sofa feeling sorry for myself, she said, 'Let's run a marathon', to which I swiftly replied, 'Let's not!'

She said I had always told her that 'out of adversity comes opportunity' and this was a perfect opportunity for us to do something: to raise money for Cancer Research UK in memory of my brother Jonathan and sister Helen.

I protested that I wasn't fit, couldn't run, wasn't in a good place. 'A marathon, for God's sake?'

Not to be put off, she swiftly entered us both for the Brighton Marathon, enthusing about just how much money we could raise for the cancer charity.

Two days later I was begrudgingly putting on an old pair of trainers and heading out for a run/walk with Sammy, puffing and panting and complaining a lot. She wouldn't stand for any of my nonsense. I said I couldn't run in my trainers, so she took me along to a running shop where I was filmed on a treadmill to make sure I purchased the right shoes for me. I was blown away by how expensive they were. I was reassured that it was money well spent because the trainers would support my feet correctly as I ran, and this would prevent injuries. I then complained that the car fumes were too much for me and I couldn't breathe, so it was impossible for me to run. So she mapped out our training routes along private roads and in parks. That stopped me using the car fumes excuse. My next complaint was that I needed music to run with. So Sammy very kindly took time to make me a playlist for my iPhone. Of course, that wasn't good enough for me: I complained that it was 'the wrong kind of music, I can't possibly run to it'.

It was only after one particular day, when we were out running and I was moaning like a petulant child and she ran off and left me, that I realised I was being awful to her and needed to change my frame of mind. Thankfully she returned ten minutes later … stopped … put her hands on her hips … looked at me angrily and asked, 'Are you doing this or what?' I sheepishly apologised and started running slowly alongside her.

From that moment on I told as many people as I could that I was going to run a marathon. I wasn't surprised many of them wondered how I would actually be able to do that, bearing in mind my weight and state of mind. Plus I was in my early fifties, not really a time when people embark on their first ever marathon. The important thing was, the more people I told, the less likely I was to chicken out. I wouldn't want to lose face by not doing it.

Slowly we got fitter and fitter. Surprisingly I actually enjoyed the training and the long runs. I began to feel good about myself and what we were going to achieve. Some of the people I told even began believing I might actually be able to do this because they could see my determination. Every day I told myself, 'You can run a marathon', hoping I would eventually believe that I could. I felt more empowered every day I trained, spurred on by the fact that people were being so generous with their sponsorship.

I now took the training very seriously. We were following a book called *The Non-Runner's Marathon Trainer*. It is aimed at people like me who are unfit and have never contemplated running a marathon before. It promises to get you to the point where you can actually finish a marathon. I was yet to be convinced when I started the sixteen-week training schedule. I remember one section, very early on, that said if you feel pain, say to yourself, 'Run with me, pain.' Well, all I could think at the time was, 'That's a load of rubbish, I just want the pain in my side to stop, I'm not running with it.' The more I worked through the programme, the more it made sense, and I loved the training by the end and felt ready for the 26.2 miles.

The day came for the Brighton Marathon and I was so nervous. Our friend Bob, who had run a few marathons, got up at the crack of dawn and came down from London to support us on the start line, which meant a lot to us both. He knew that feeling of trepidation at the start, and wanted us to know that all the training would kick in and that the feeling as we crossed the finish line would be amazing.

I was up for it. After all I had been through in the last few years, I was eager to really challenge myself, both mentally and physically, and to raise money in memory of my brother and sister. It felt good. As Sammy and I started running across the start line with the hundreds of other runners beside us it felt surreal. I felt very tearful and overwhelmed as well as excited. Sammy reminded me to start off slowly, not to rush with the excitement of it all, because I would burn out too soon. She said, 'Remember, Mum, pace yourself and you've got this.' After a mile or so I lost sight of her in the distance and I just kept calm and remembered my training tips. The support of family and friends along the way was incredible. It is amazing how one minute you are flagging then you suddenly hear a familiar voice in the distance shouting your name and you look up and feel so re-energised.

I was genuinely surprised how good I felt at the halfway mark. It was the last few miles that were a struggle, mainly because I had this fear of 'hitting the wall', something so many people talk about: when you struggle to run near the end of the marathon. I just kept saying to myself, 'Stopping is not an option, stopping is not an option', over and over again, and somehow it got me through. As I approached the finish line, on Brighton seafront, I could hear my family screaming, 'Come on, Siobhan! Come on, Siobhan!' It was very emotional. I started to cry as I ran the last few hundred yards to the finish line. Even writing this now brings tears to my eyes and I feel goosebumps all over. At the time I was so proud of myself. My daughter was already at the finish line, wrapped in her silver blanket, waiting for me. My heart swelled when I saw her big smile, willing me to cross it too. I ran the last few hundred yards on cloud nine. Seeing her and listening to the emotional cries from my brother's and sister's families was amazing. It is hard to put into words how I felt crossing that finish line. I honestly felt like I was a superwoman and that I could achieve anything I put my mind to.

Why could I not do that in other areas of my life? Why did I allow myself to accept being treated unfairly? Why did I not feel strong enough to speak out?

I then had the realisation that the only person who was going to stop me being strong and challenging ageism and unfairness was me. That was a very empowering moment and one I will never forget. It made me even more determined to embark on an adventure and find a way of ageing as positively as I could. But what would that adventure be?

Chapter 2

Taking on the World

I had already had a taste of adventure in my late forties when Sammy was going to university. I was facing the prospect of being on my own again. I had just undergone a hysterectomy (I call it my 'hystericalectomy', because I have never been the same since) because I had precancerous cells. As a result of the operation I went straight into a full surgical menopause. It was awful. I felt so lost and depressed, not only recovering from major surgery but also not knowing what was going on with my emotions and body. I had thought the menopause was mainly about your periods stopping and hot flushes. I hadn't a clue about the impact it would have on me. I suffered with aching joints and felt weepy, anxious and forgetful. Initially I decided to try to navigate the menopause without the help of hormone replacement therapy (HRT), especially as I had been told at the time it could possibly be linked to breast cancer. That is now very much up for debate. It wasn't long, though, before I realised I needed HRT if I was going to live my life. So I began taking the tablets.

Even with HRT I experienced periods of feeling very low, which was difficult for Sammy. I went from being the life and soul of a party to spending hours and hours lying on the sofa unable to do anything, including getting a shower some days. I also piled on the weight. I became increasingly angry with everyone and everything. I hated the way I looked and felt. My daughter has since told me that she would compare notes with friends in the sixth form about their mothers' behaviour and they all came to the conclusion, before we did, that it was caused by the menopause. I was oblivious to the impact it was having on her.

I began making excuses rather than going out with friends, and instead I stayed in bed, ate rubbish and slept for hours. It was so far away from my usual way of living, but I could not get myself together. When I had to, I could paint my face on and pretend, then collapse into a heap when I had used up all my energy pretending, just to make others happy. I got sick of pretending and just felt numb and that I was on the outside looking in on life.

I would save my energy to go to work, where it was a struggle to get through the day. Despite it only being a fifteen-minute walk to work, I would get a taxi because I felt so exhausted. When I got home after a long ten-hour shift, I would have a bowl of cereal for dinner and then go straight to bed. I had no energy for anything else.

When I look back I feel so sad that I felt the need to hide it. I convinced myself that I couldn't let people know, and so I didn't turn to family or friends for help. I felt like a failure because I wasn't coping. I did go to the doctor, though, many times. Some of the male doctors made me feel like I was wasting their time; one said I might have fibromyalgia. I remember crying to them saying, 'I'm too young to feel this bad, this tired and weak.' I knew it was having an impact at work too, where I felt too emotional and vulnerable to stand up for myself. I had to take sick days off just to sleep all day to try to stem the feelings of exhaustion.

Sometimes I wished I had cancer so I could give them a solid reason for why I felt so bad.

It all changed when a young female doctor put me on oestrogen gel, which I rub into my arms every morning. After a few weeks I began to feel like my old self, and years later I still use it to manage my symptoms.

It was not long after my hysterectomy that my brother Jonathan died; both of these things so close together left me struggling at work. I also felt more invisible and voiceless the older I became. I would think back to when I was younger and how happy I had felt travelling in India and Nepal, trekking in the Himalaya. I wanted to feel that kind of happiness again. I wanted to travel again. The problem was, I had a mortgage and bills to pay. I had a well-paid, secure job and I was nowhere near being able to retire. So how on earth could I make it happen? I would watch travel programmes on TV, dreaming of being able to travel to those far-flung places myself one day.

After numerous sleepless nights tossing and turning, mulling over so many possible scenarios in my head, I woke up one morning with an idea that really excited me. I would put my gorgeous three-bedroom terraced house in Tunbridge Wells up for sale. If it sold then that would be a sign. Much to my amazement, it sold within the week, for the top asking price. The couple buying it loved it so much they asked me to take it off the market straight away. I remember being overwhelmed with fear because I knew that now I had no excuse not to go ahead and plan my adventure.

A few days later I plucked up the courage to go to my boss and ask if there was any chance I could take a gap year from work. I explained that I was struggling with life and needed time out, but that I didn't want to leave my job. I had to wait several anxious weeks before he called me into his office. I remember my heart pounding in my chest. I knew that in the next few minutes I would know if I could break free from my life for a while or if my dreams would be shattered. I sat down and just looked across the room at him. When I saw a smile break on his face I began to feel emotional because I was filled with hope. I don't remember exactly what he said to me in that moment, except that my request for a gap year had been approved by the human resources department. I remember his lips moving as he continued talking, but inside I was going crazy. I just wanted to run out of the room screaming to everyone that I was finally able to go on my gap year!

Logistically it was a bit of a nightmare to sort, including getting my daughter to university and buying her a car so that she would be able to see her father in the holidays, as I would not be around. It also made me feel less guilty about the fact that I was heading off the moment she went to uni. It took time to finalise the sale of the house and my car. Thankfully one of my friends had a massive garage and let me store most of my belongings in there. The rest I divided out amongst friends who held on to it all for me for the year. Many of those friends had seen how I had been struggling with life the past year or so and were excited for me heading off on this adventure. They also thought I was crazy to be doing it as I approached fifty and asked if I was scared to be going alone. That was what was exciting me, making me feel alive: the prospect of a solo adventure.

Next step was to get myself a round-the-world air ticket. That was far trickier than I had envisaged, compounded by the fact that I wasn't sure exactly where I wanted to go, or how best to plan a route. It was time to call in the experts. After five hours in Trailfinders in Brighton I came out with a ticket that suited my needs. I would fly to large cities and then sort out travel arrangements locally. The ticket took me from London to Bangkok, Bangkok to Sydney, Sydney to Auckland, Auckland to Suva in Fiji, Suva to Vancouver, Vancouver to São Paulo and finally São Paulo back to London.

* * *

I was so excited to board the plane to Bangkok at Heathrow in November 2007, at the grand old age of forty-eight. I sat on the plane in tears thinking, 'Oh my goodness, this is really happening.' I admit that at the time I was overcome with fear about what lay ahead, coupled with lots and lots of excitement about the prospect of backpacking solo around the world for the next year. No more worrying about pleasing other people. Just time for me to regroup. Prior to my departure I had been bombarded by comments from everyone: 'You're so brave! I couldn't do that', 'Won't you get lonely?', 'Aren't you scared?', 'My husband wouldn't let me do that', 'I'd love to do what you're doing.' All these were swirling round in my head now, just adding to my heightened emotions. It is no wonder I didn't really settle on the long flight. It may also have been because it was an extremely bumpy flight. Eventually we landed in Bangkok. My midlife adventure had really begun. This was my mature gap year.

The first few nights in Bangkok were strange. I felt a bit numb and directionless. I had booked myself into a good hotel thinking that that was a sensible move so that I could find my bearings and be safe. In retrospect it was a mistake. The problem was, it was pretty soulless. The room looked just like any other hotel room anywhere in the world. I thought to myself, 'What have I done?' I even questioned whether I had made a mistake altogether travelling alone. I wanted more of an interactive experience; to get more involved in the local culture and meet interesting people by experiencing their lives with homestays and staying in local hostels, a far cry from my generic hotel room.

It was only when I started immersing myself into everything, like the chaotic, cramped local transport, staying in hostels and getting internal flights to the neighbouring islands, that I started to settle into my nomadic life. At times it was challenging, but I loved it and felt alive overcoming many challenges: bartering for a tuk-tuk, stressing that I didn't want to be taken miles out of my way to look at their friend's carpet shop; deciphering menus written in the local language. I was beginning to leave the worries of work behind me and to focus on really enjoying taking in my surroundings.

I loved hanging out with people of all ages. From day one in Krabi I got talking to a group of Canadians in their teens and twenties at a barbecue organised on the roof of one of the hostels. Even though I was old enough to be their mother they didn't care and they made me feel so welcome. I remember at the time writing in my blog that they thought I was ten years younger than I actually was, and I was thrilled with that. Nowadays my outlook on life has completely changed. I would gently say to them, 'Thank you so much, I know you mean that as a compliment but this is what a forty-eight-year-old woman looks like. I don't want to look younger than I am because old is good too.' Society says that we should look a certain way in our forties, fifties, sixties and beyond, but we all age differently and we should just try to embrace that, not strive to look younger. I don't need to look younger to feel good about myself. I can be old and still look amazing. Being with that group, though, was the first time I knew that age doesn't really matter. It is the people you are with and how you interact with them, not what age they are. They didn't care that I was nearly thirty years older than them; in their minds I was just fun to be with. They even sought out my company on the islands of Koh Phi Phi and Koh Samui, and in Australia months later.

I loved my time in Thailand, Laos, Cambodia and Vietnam, seeing all the places I had longed to visit for many years. As I spent time backpacking I could feel my self-confidence grow, and I loved the feeling of freedom and going with the flow. It was so stimulating just spending time with people. One particular memory is sitting chatting with Buddhist monks in Luang Prabang, in Laos, so that they could practise their English and I could learn more about their way of life. I felt totally at peace and grateful that I had the time to just sit and really connect with them, rather than having to rush off somewhere to do something. They also made me feel good about myself, something I realised I had not felt for many years.

Other highlights were watching the sunrise from the top of the steep temple steps at Angkor Wat in Cambodia; spending four days navigating the wondrous Mekong River from Thailand to Laos in a rickety, long wooden boat, with lots of other travellers and locals. There was no health and safety: I just had to clamber aboard, over very choppy waters, along a very long, bendy plank, with my heavy rucksack on my back. Even that gave me such a sense of achievement at the time. I felt so nimble, a stark contrast with a few weeks earlier, at the start of my trip in Thailand. I had fallen head first into the sea with my rucksack on my back because my knees gave way when I jumped off a boat transporting us to an island. I had let my fitness levels go and my knees weren't as strong as I thought. I didn't hurt myself, just my pride, and I knew I had to get fitter. The only low I had in South East Asia was losing my nice warm jacket on the border between Cambodia and Vietnam, only to find that it was the coldest it had been in Vietnam in forty years, and I was freezing. I searched around for days to find somewhere to buy a warmer jacket. One lady at a market stall took one look at me and said in earnest, 'Oh no, we no do big size!' It left me feeling very deflated as I had never thought of myself as a 'big size', but compared to Vietnamese people I suppose I am.

I was so ready for the sunshine of Australia. During my three months exploring there I certainly did get fitter. There were lots of healthy juice bars for me to get daily juices. I walked for miles along the cliffs at Bondi Beach to Coogee Beach, enjoying watching the surfers waiting for that perfect wave. I never had the urge to give it a go myself, though.

I went to stay in Melbourne with a couple I had befriended on the beautiful Thai island of Koh Phi Phi. I had been walking along a beach one evening and sneezed, and I heard a voice say, 'Bless you.' I turned around and got chatting, and we struck up a fabulous friendship. They kindly took some of the winter clothes I was lugging around and told me I could collect them when I came to stay.

Sammy flew out to meet me in Melbourne when I was staying with them. The only problem was that I had got the plane times wrong. I had been out the night before with my Australian friends and we were a bit slow off the mark to head to the airport. I was convinced we still had plenty of time before she landed. As we were on the highway, my phone rang. I answered it to hear Sammy on the other end of the line going, 'Hi Mum, where are you?' I was mortified that I wasn't at the airport to meet her. Jokingly she loves to tell everyone, 'I flew to the other side of the world to be reunited with my mother on her mature gap year and she wasn't even there at the airport to meet me because she'd been out on the lash the night before.' Our lives really are like *Ab Fab*: she's Saffy and I'm Eddie. I had lots of making up to do when I did eventually get to the airport fifteen minutes later. I just threw my arms around her and cried. I was so happy to see her. We had six wonderful weeks backpacking around Australia together. We even climbed Sydney Harbour Bridge with her cousin Carmel, who had lived in Sydney for several years. It was heart-wrenching to say my goodbyes to her in Brisbane as she headed back to university. We have such a close bond between us.

* * *

I was really beginning to reconnect with my life, and even more so in New Zealand, where I walked for miles on beautiful beaches as I explored both islands. I climbed a glacier and did a tandem skydive from 1,300 feet. I had joked with friends in one of the hostels that if the only way to get near a fella was by strapping myself to him and jumping out of a plane at 1,300 feet, then I would do it, not thinking for a moment anyone would take me seriously. Before I knew it, the next day I was heading off in the plane to do the skydive. It was amazing, one of the best things I have ever done. I would certainly do it again.

After all the adrenaline rushes that New Zealand had to offer, I was quite happy to relax on the wonderfully peaceful Fijian islands. They were mind-blowingly beautiful. I headed for the Yasawa islands, which have the most immaculate sun-drenched, white beaches and clear, warm, turquoise seas. I began to value the small pleasures again. I stayed in huts with the locals and totally escaped from life; I sat with them under the coconut trees and listened to their tales of island life. I also had plenty of time to reflect on my life. I swam in the clear waters and wandered for miles alone with my thoughts. I found my inner peace. I would get up very early and decamp to a hammock strung between two trees and lazily watch the sunrise, before someone in the distance would blow a conch shell to summon us to breakfast. I also feasted on freshly caught fish with the locals at their spontaneous barbecues along the beach. Often we played a game of volleyball. I was so rubbish at serving the ball they would look at me with pity and insist I have several attempts to get it over the net. A month later I had vastly improved and even enjoyed getting a chance to serve.

By the time I was on the last stage of my mature gap year I felt I had found my place in the world again. I knew that my voyage of discovery was working. I was excited to share that energy with my sister-in-law Maggie and her friend Sinead, who came out to join me and to explore South America.

We were all approaching fifty and they too were eager to experience what it was like to be ageless and to just travel around freely.

We did all the touristy things like seeing the Christ the Redeemer statue in Rio de Janeiro and also visited the favelas, slums run by criminals and groups of drug traffickers. We crossed into Argentina, where we saw the most amazing tango performance at an Art Deco theatre.

For me the highlight was seeing the Iguazu Falls. They make up the largest waterfall system in the world. I was struck by the roar of the water as we approached them. I was so excited even before seeing them and was not disappointed when I turned a corner and there they were. The torrent of water cascading over the falls was incredible.

The twenty-two-hour bus journey from Iguazu to Bolivia was not quite so enjoyable, though, even with reclining beds. We did manage to sleep a bit, but I was desperate for a long walk when we arrived at the banks of Lake Titicaca.

I have wanted to visit Lake Titicaca ever since I heard a teacher talking about it at primary school. I don't know why. I think I just loved the sound of the name, and it has fascinated me ever since. I had watched so many programmes about it and here I was, finally on its shores. It straddles the border between Peru and Bolivia in the Andes. It is one of South America's largest lakes and the world's highest navigable body of water. It didn't disappoint. It also helped that this last year of travel had enabled me to stop, relax and take in my surroundings more than I used to.

I discovered one of my favourite tipples on the floating islands near Puno: a pisco sour cocktail. I loved it! The name comes from the base liquor pisco and the citrus juice and sweetener added to it. To this day every time I have one it takes me back to the fab times on my gap year.

Finally we undertook the Lares Trek in Peru. I wanted to end my mature gap year on a high. Literally. The Lares Trek is one of the main alternatives to the Inca Trail. It is a far quieter four-day, high-altitude hike from just outside Cusco to Machu Picchu.

It was hard going in the heavy rain and freezing temperatures, and I did struggle with my breathing a bit at around 4,400 metres above sea level. But it was all worth it for the views across the Peruvian Andes and for the locals we met along the way.

On one particular day of the walk I had a pounding headache and was worried that I was getting altitude sickness. The guides gave me coca leaves to put in my cheek to chew as I was walking. It was really effective; my headache subsided. Coca leaves are sacred to the Incas as they use them as natural remedies.

The guides and porters who accompanied us worked so hard to erect our tents for the night and to produce the most delicious meals high up in the mountains. It was magical. I would sit around chatting with the other people on the expedition about what had led us all to this wonderful experience together. I shared a tent with a woman from New Zealand. She too had had a bit of burnout in her life and wanted to take a step off the corporate ladder for a while to regroup. She was intrigued to hear my story and how I was now near the end of my journey, ready to face my everyday life again. We got on really well. We would be in fits of laughter before we eventually settled down for the night. Being so high up above sea level, it was very, very cold at night. As a consequence we put on the lovely colourful hats with ear flaps that we had purchased in Cusco, plus several layers of clothes, including thick, woolly jumpers. We looked ridiculous but we were determined not to be cold. There was one problem with our strategy, though: when we had to venture out to the toilet tent in the night, there were so many thermal layers to get through it took ages to have a pee.

I thoroughly enjoyed my time in South America and felt the benefits of taking time out for myself. I also realised the benefits of having far fewer belongings. During the last twelve months I had managed well with the contents of my rucksack, which I repacked, cleaned and decluttered regularly. I would even discover items I had actually forgotten I had. I just learnt to put on what was clean, and it worked. I hoped to be more minimalistic when I returned home.

Of course, Sammy was on time to meet me when I arrived at the airport!

At the end of my mature gap year I felt ageless. I also felt the seed had been sown for me to travel and to champion positive ageing when I eventually retired.

I hoped I would be able to take my new-found confidence and the feeling of agelessness into my everyday life now that I was going back to work.

Chapter 3

The London Marathon, Yorkshire Three Peaks and Malawi

Over the next few years I settled back into my life in Tunbridge Wells, working for the local TV regional news programme. I found myself a lovely flat near the Pantiles area, which is a beautiful part of town. It has a colonnaded walkway that was developed in the seventeenth century and has been a popular tourist attraction since the discovery of the Chalybeate Spring.

After I finished the Brighton Marathon I intended to retire at the peak of what I classed as my marathon career. I was happy to have crossed the finish line in five hours two minutes and pleased that we had raised so much money for charity. Sammy, on the other hand, had other ideas. She entered me into the London Marathon ballot. My friends told me not to worry because the odds are pretty slim of getting a place in the first ballot you enter. I arrived home from work one day and saw a large brown envelope. I just stared at it because I could see who it was from. I actually prayed that it was a rejection letter. Well, you guessed it: when I opened it, I saw the word 'congratulations'.

I had only gone and got myself a place in the 2014 London Marathon, at fifty-five years old. I burst into tears and just thought, 'Oh no, I can't go through all that training again.' This soon turned to Yorkshire grit and a determination deep inside me that said, 'You've done this before, you can do it again – and raise money for a good cause.'

The irony was that Sammy didn't get a place. I spent the next day calling around lots of charities and saying that I would run for them if they gave my daughter a place. I said that we had a good track record of raising money for cancer research. Finally Children with Cancer UK gave her a place.

This time I had to undergo the training on my own because Sammy had gone to live in London with her boyfriend. Once again I told everyone I could that I was going to run the London Marathon so that I wouldn't drop out. I followed the same book I'd used before: a sixteen-week programme that increases the length of the long runs each week. I remember watching the little snowdrops and daffodils popping up through the soil on my training. Each week I loved seeing them surface and eventually bloom in the spring sunshine as I got nearer to the day of the marathon.

It was a great feeling going to collect our numbers a few days before. It was then that I found out my starting gate was the blue one: the same one the elite athletes use, Mo Farah included. All my family and friends found this hilarious. Obviously Mo would have gone way before I dragged myself over the start line, but it didn't stop me dining out on the fact that I was an elite athlete starter at the marathon.

It was a tremendous day. I just kept crying as I ran past various landmarks like the *Cutty Sark*, Tower Bridge and Canary Wharf.

Once again the crowds were wonderful, cheering me on and helping me get to the finish line. The bit by Buckingham Palace is confusing because I thought I just had to go around a corner and it was the home straight to the finish line, but there are a few little bends before the final straight section on The Mall. I was totally wiped out but elated when I crossed the finish line, this time in about five hours nine minutes. I was glad to be alive. I spent a while trying to find Sammy, as she had finished before me. It was very emotional when we saw one another. We flung our arms around each other and cried. We were marathoners once more and it felt like such a tremendous achievement. This, though, would definitely be my last.

Once again it gave me renewed strength to face life. All the pressures at work and in everyday life in my mid- to late fifties did still overwhelm me at times, and I knew that I needed to dig deep and use this strength to sort my life out.

The more I struggled with the menopause and finding my place in society in my late fifties, the more I needed to challenge myself. I knew running the marathons had boosted my mental well-being. So a couple of years later I embarked on the Yorkshire Three Peaks Challenge with some relatives from Canada and other members of my family.

My younger brother Paddy coordinated things for us. I found us a hostel to stay in near Pen-y-ghent. When we opened the door to go inside we were immediately hit by a wall of warm air and the horrible stench of sweat and body odour. A man was shaking his head at us, as if to indicate maybe we should look for something else, as there were a bunch of them already established in the room. Thankfully there was a nice hotel down the road with enough room for us. We didn't sleep well, though, because we were excited about the next day's adventure. We got up very early and rendezvoused at my brother's motorhome, not far from the start. He was used to organising things like this after years as an officer in the military. We got a thorough briefing on the health and safety measures and the route. Then after breakfasting on a big bowl of porridge we headed off, at the crack of dawn, to climb Pen-y-ghent, Whernside and Ingleborough, hopefully in twelve hours.

I foolishly had bought some new boots not long before and, as my brother told me, I hadn't broken them in very well, so they started to rub pretty soon into the walk. I had also way overpacked my rucksack, so I was lugging far too much weight with me. All this slowed me down and made the whole thing far harder than it should have been. We ended up finishing the day in just over thirteen hours. My brother must have predicted this because when we were in the pub afterwards he presented us all with personalised certificates he had made to show that we had at least completed the Yorkshire Three Peaks Challenge, albeit taking a little longer than the required twelve hours for the official certificate.

It is still to this day one of the hardest things I have ever done. I completed it more through grit and determination than physical aptitude. My brother often says that he was impressed with me digging deep and getting on with it even though my boots were killing me.

For me this is also a reflection of a lot of aspects of my life: just digging deep and getting on with it no matter what life throws at me. Talking to women throughout my travels, that is also a state of mind a lot of them can relate to in midlife. I've often been told that what I have done is courageous. But it is circumstances that have forced me to be courageous. Many times I had no choice but to soldier on.

Despite being able to challenge myself physically, I still struggled very much with my self-esteem and identity in the workplace. I was losing myself. Plus I felt that society was getting more ageist, particularly in the workplace, where older people who have so much to offer are often undervalued and overlooked. Many feel they have no option but to leave work earlier than they would have liked. I didn't like what I was seeing and experiencing. I wanted to support women who felt the same way I did. I wanted to encourage them to have adventures.

So I put together a talk called 'Ageless, Fearless Women: You Can Do It Too' and gave it at a women's conference attended by over 500 women in Kent. That was the first time I had voiced my plans to retire, buy a motorhome and go travelling around Great Britain, challenging ageism and championing positive ageing. The idea of a motorhome had literally popped into my head one morning, and the more I thought about it the more I liked the idea. It excited me, especially as I had never ever holidayed in one or driven one, so I'm not sure why it seemed like a solution to being free, but it was the perfect escape plan from my current way of life. My route to adventure. It just made perfect sense for me to become a nomad. I was also going to get rid of most of my possessions because I was becoming increasingly disenchanted with how we live our lives. People work long hours to buy STUFF to fill their houses. They need to earn the money to pay for all that STUFF, which in turn means they don't spend quality time with family and friends. They have to fit people in when they have a window in their calendar. They may have had a horrendous week and are shattered, but they have to see their friends because that is the only time they can fit them in. And when they do see them they're tired and just go through the motions, glad when they've gone home, which is sad. There's no quality time there. I wanted to show that we can live with far less stuff and connect more so as to be happier in our old age.

At that conference I was asked by a group of women to join them on an entrepreneurial expedition to Malawi to meet local women setting up businesses and banks to improve their quality of life. I jumped at the chance because I am very much about women supporting women.

I was blown away by the experience, seeing just how different their lives are and how women support other women to create simple businesses and loan schemes that they can really use to improve their lives. One charity we supported made washable sanitary pads for girls who couldn't afford to buy sanitary products. Each month when they were menstruating they would have to take time off school, missing out on vital educa-tion. By giving them reusable sanitary towels they could continue to go to school and so have a better chance of staying in education, thus improving their future prospects in life.

Being fifty-nine, it was also time for me to undergo another physical challenge, which was why I agreed to join the group to climb Mount Mulanje, the highest mountain in Malawi. It was an incredible bonding experience for us all in the searing forty-degree heat. Many of the group were approaching sixty and we compared how we had all been dealing with the menopause. It was also interesting to hear how many were experiencing ageism in their workplaces. Some spoke about their experiences of being bullied and how older women were being forced out.

I was determined somehow when I retired to try and address these things.

I remember on a bus trip in Malawi talking to one particular woman called Sam, who ran a running group for older women in Sevenoaks, about my plans to retire at sixty, get rid of my possessions and buy a motorhome and travel Great Britain in it, having never driven or even holidayed in a motorhome before. We both laughed at the prospect of my crazy idea. Even then I wasn't sure exactly how I was going to do it, but I knew I had to do it to find my happy place. And to inspire other women not to give up when life gets tough, but to find a new path for the next phase of their lives.

Chapter 4

This Is Really Happening

As I approached my sixtieth birthday I felt the pressure of impending retirement with a mixture of trepidation and a lot of excitement. One thing I did know, though, was that I was ready for it. I wanted to live my life on my terms. I wanted to break the stereotype of retired pensioners; to be part of a movement that encourages a more positive representation of growing old in retirement. I wanted to see more positive images of courageous, strong, beautiful women in their sixties and beyond. Not wrinkled hands or white-haired, frail individuals. I would show that old can be beautiful and vibrant. For many of the friends and women I connect with on social media, it is a time when they are finding themselves. They are living through numerous adventures and challenges. I am pro-age. As a 'retirement rebel' I would be lobbying to change the negative narratives associated with ageing. I still wasn't really sure how I would go about doing that at this stage. Mainly I wanted to promote a more positive slant on this phase of life and to stop women feeling lost.

I know that I had chosen early retirement, but I wasn't sure how I would actually cope with life away from my job. It had given me a sense of identity and a purpose for the last thirty years. Just how easy would it be for me to shrug off that identity? I was a bit rudderless. At times I was even afraid of what my future held for me.

Choosing to give up a good job and a regular salary for a very unpredictable life on the road just seemed to confirm to people that I was a bit mad. When I talked about it at work people would say to me, 'Oh my goodness, you're actually going to do this, aren't you?' They would ask, 'Aren't you scared?' to which I would reply, 'Yes, but that's half the fun.' This only reaffirmed to them that I was crazy. They would also add, though, that they were jealous and wished they too had the courage to head off in a motorhome and see where life took them.

Truthfully, I had no idea then where my life was going to take me.

Before I had even put my plan into action my new boss threw a spanner in the works. He called me into his office and asked if I wanted to reconsider my retirement options, as he would like to get me out reporting again: something I had wanted to do for a long time, which made it very tempting indeed to stay. I went home that night and spent the weekend in a quandary, swinging from 'Okay, I'll stay another year' to 'No, I'm going to retire because I've dreamt about retirement and travel for so long. I need to find myself and live my life differently. I'm too stressed out.'

I could no longer carry on working in the environment I was in. I needed to find my voice and to help other women who felt the same way I did to find theirs too. Time and time again throughout my fifties I had shown myself that I could achieve things physically: running two marathons and climbing the

Yorkshire Three Peaks and Mount Mulanje. Yet I felt so lost and anxious in my everyday life. I often just went through the motions to keep others happy. I wasn't feeling the joy of things. It was time for change. It was time to retire now and there was no turning back. I was ready to really start trusting in life to see where it took me.

I wanted to take steps now towards the life of my dreams.

On the Monday I went into my boss's office and said, 'I'm thrilled that you value me enough to want me to reconsider retirement, but I've not made my decision lightly. So many things have led me to feeling that this is the right time: bereavements, medical worries, work pressures.' I added, 'I feel like I'm at the edge of a cliff about to jump into the greatest adventure of my life and I'm ready to jump. Yes, it is scary and I have no idea where I am going to land, but I know I have to do it now.' I knew that I needed to go to the edge to feel alive. I believed that this was the only route for me to find the inner peace and happiness I longed for. I didn't want to live my life stressed and miserable. There had to be a better, more positive way for me to grow old. If there was, I wanted to show other women that with courage you can go from feeling lost in life to finding your voice and becoming what you want to be.

He told me he was sorry I wasn't staying but that he totally understood that I wanted to go. I clearly remember walking out of his office that day into the newsroom and being overwhelmed with happiness; I looked around at everyone, knowing that I had made the right decision. I was so excited about the next stage of my life, my next adventure.

* * *

That night I spent hours searching for my perfect motorhome online, until the early hours of the morning.

'What will my future home look like?' 'Will I be able to afford the kind of motorhome that I love?' 'Will I be able to drive it around?' 'Will life in the motorhome be how I expect it to be?' 'Will I find my happy place?' It was all well and good talking about it, but doing it would be another matter. A challenge that I was excited to take on …

When the idea first popped into my head to get a motorhome for my retirement travels, I was a bit bemused because I had never holidayed in one. The nearest I had come to it was when I was backpacking solo around the world and became friends with a young couple in New Zealand. They invited me to sleep in their four-berth motorhome one night on South Island. It would take me lots of searching, though, from the epiphany moment of realising a motorhome was the answer to my prayers, to finding the one that would become my home.

It is a minefield trying to find the right motorhome. There is a sea of possibilities, with so many different designs, coupled with the fact that I really was letting my heart rule my head. Somehow I felt that I would instinctively know when I found the right one. I also found out that everyone who knows about motorhomes has an opinion about the best layout, what you might need, etc. Some swear by having a bed that is made up all the time. Others say I must get one with a 'garage'. You access that from the side of the vehicle and usually it is the dead space under a fixed bed, so you get the benefit of a fixed bed and space to store things.

I chatted to my brother Paddy and his wife, Lorraine, who have owned several motorhomes and love holidaying in them.

They were very supportive about my idea and gave me the benefit of their experiences. They told me to get one with plenty of storage space, as I would get frustrated if I had to keep moving things out of the shower and toilet cubicle every time I parked up. They said they got frustrated making up a bed every night so they have now opted for a fixed bed. Personally I knew that making up a bed for one every night wouldn't bother me. I'd rather have more room during the day to move about. Their advice did help me make a final decision on what would work for me as a home.

Eventually the day came to physically go and start looking for my house on wheels. My good friend Hamish, who knew even less than me about motorhomes, agreed to accompany me on my search. We spent over five hours driving around various dealerships.

At first we were both quite giggly because we were stepping in and out of these motorhomes not really having a clue what we were looking for. Pretty quickly, though, we were saying, 'Oh no, do not like that', or 'Oh, this one feels good, now this could be a possibility.' I have to say it was also a reality check for me, seeing what I would get for my money. They turned out to be a lot more expensive than I had initially envisaged, especially the types I was favouring. I knew I wanted something that made me, feel like I was stepping into a homely space; a space that made sense to me, with kitchen and bathroom areas, central heating and plenty of room to have friends over for meals.

After much deliberation and hours and hours of searching, over many months, I narrowed it down to two motorhomes I had seen online: one in Kent and one in Banbury. I travelled up to Banbury. The moment I stepped into it I knew I wanted it.

It is a two-berth Auto-Trail Tribute 615, with the perfect layout for my future as a nomadic retirement rebel. It has long bench seats either side that pull out into beds, so I could have two single beds, one either side, or join them together to make one massive bed across the width of the motorhome. It has all the mod cons: oven, hob, grill, fridge-freezer, microwave, central heating that runs off gas and electricity, full-size shower, toilet and sink. The front two seats swivel around to provide lovely armchairs to relax in. I knew that this motorhome would give me the freedom to create a life uniquely tailored to me, to give me that sense of authenticity I had been craving for so long. It also had very low mileage and was within my budget of £40,000.

I was ecstatic. It looked good as new and it had been owned by an elderly couple who hardly used it.

I haggled a bit with the price and managed to get a few thousand off and a few extras added in like gas cylinders, tax and a full tank of petrol. I was taking a risk that I might not have got it right, but I was willing to take that risk. I decided it was time to put my money where my mouth was and hand over the deposit. I arranged to pick it up a few weeks later, after I had left work and sorted my flat and belongings. I literally cried with joy as I drove away from the dealership. I was the proud owner of a motorhome and my adventure was taking shape.

* * *

My last day at work finally arrived. I woke up and decided I wanted to look my best for my final shift. I put on my pretty blue flowery dress and applied my makeup as if I were going to a wedding. I felt good about myself, and I looked at myself in

the bedroom mirror and said out loud, 'This is it, Siobhan …
the next phase of your life is about to begin … You've got this,
girl.' I knew that this was a time in my life when I couldn't ignore
what I needed to make me happy. We only have one shot at this
living lark, and I was going to give it my best. There was an
ocean of possibilities out there for me to be who I always should
have been before life got in the way. I phoned Sammy and we
chatted about how significant the day was and what an exciting
phase of my life I had in front of me. I told her I had butterflies
in my stomach. As usual she calmed me down and told me how
excited she was for me and wished me luck.

The July sun was shining as I walked up the high street in
Tunbridge Wells towards the office, a walk I had undertaken for
the last ten years. I savoured every moment, knowing that from
today my life was going to change for good. I smiled to myself
in anticipation. I wanted to shout out loud for all the shop-
keepers and owners to hear, 'This is my last walk to work, soon
I will be free! Free to do what I want, when I want!' Thankfully
I restrained myself and just enjoyed the walk.

I didn't do much work that day, to be honest. I spent the day
saying my goodbyes, emptying my locker and relishing the
feeling of throwing away my notebooks and all the detritus
I'd accumulated over the years. There was already someone
hovering to grab my locker when I'd finished. I was presented
with flowers and presents, which included a year's membership
of the Caravan and Motorhome Club. I loved the mug they
gave me with my personal logo on it: a picture of a motorhome with my face superimposed on it and the word
'SHUVONSHUVOFF', which is what I'd chosen to call my
blog. I had planned to say all kinds of things in a goodbye speech.

To my surprise I could hardly say anything. I just teared up and felt very emotional, but thankfully I did manage a few words between the tears.

A group of us headed to a bar on the Pantiles to celebrate the end of one chapter and the start of another, with several bottles of bubbly. And so my retirement rebellion began.

Chapter 5

Packing Up

I had an incredible party in the garden of my flat at the end of July 2019 to mark my sixtieth birthday, retirement and my shuvonshuvoff adventure. I decorated the garden like a mini music festival, with bunting, balloons and lanterns strung up in the trees and bushes, keeping my fingers crossed that the rain would hold off, as I didn't have a plan B if the heavens did open. I placed seating, rugs and cushions all around the garden for people to just relax and listen to the music. A local band came and built a fab little stage so that they could play alongside musical friends. We were serenaded and we danced well into the night. It had a really laid-back feeling with people coming and going throughout. I loved having my family and friends around me. I was well known for throwing get-togethers and dinner parties throughout the years and I did worry that I would miss this interaction in my new life. But only time would tell. I had felt for a long time that I needed to break free from my current way of life. It was time for me to take back my autonomy and to find my inner power and inner peace. I wanted to re-emerge with a renewed strength and love of life. I just felt that the sooner I made changes in my life, the better my life would be.

If it didn't work out, it wasn't irreversible. This party was a great way to draw a line in the sand and to move forward with so much love and goodwill from everyone.

Many of the presents I was given supported my new lifestyle choices: St Christopher medals, a compass, travel journals and travel books to read to give me inspiration. Plus a flag on a very long pole. If I lost my motorhome on a site I could just head for the flag.

Now the partying was over it was finally time to get rid of my flat and take stock of all my STUFF: what to keep and what to get rid of. It was harder than I imagined.

I looked around and was blown away by just how much stuff I had accumulated over the years. It would never fit in my motorhome, so most of it was going to have to go. I had to make tough decisions and to start packing and deciding what was needed and what could be discarded. To be totally honest, I would have loved to just pick it all up, put it in a skip and get rid of it. If only it was that easy; but this was a lifetime of memories, of happy times and heartache, laid out on the floor.

It took me several weeks to look through the cupboards, drawers and boxes. I was transported back to good and bad times in my life. I read and reread the letters from solicitors from when I went through a particularly acrimonious break-up many years ago, when my daughter was nearly four. I was shocked at how raw my emotions became. I remember being terrified all those years ago at the prospect of being a single mother, juggling full-time work and parenting. I had to buy a home for us both and find a school for her, all of which was very, very stressful and frightening. Now I took great delight in ripping up the pages of the correspondence and throwing them in the bin bag. It was quite cathartic. I looked back and I was so proud of how I coped and how Sammy and I thrived. There were so many good memories as well: old school books of Sammy's for instance. I remember even when she was very little, we would always get the giggles sitting outside the teacher's room looking through her books on parents' evenings. Her drawings were so bad we found it funny. The teachers always enthused about what a lovely little girl she was and how she was so clever. I would burst with pride. It wasn't necessarily a perfect upbringing for Sammy. As I looked through her childhood memories, it dawned on me that she shouldered a lot for a little girl: I worked long hours, and she was often alone until I got home from work and had to get herself ready to go to school if I was on an early shift. I was often just in survival mode and getting through life, and so was she alongside me. My heart swelled and I had a little cry just thinking about it. She never gave me any trouble. She was such a good little girl. It is a credit to her that she has grown into the most incredible woman who is my friend as well as my cherished daughter.

Yes, sifting through my belongings really was an emotional rollercoaster. When I looked through my visitors' book, which people had filled in over the years when they came to stay, I noticed several entries from my sister Helen. It made me miss her so much, and also my mother, who had died only four months earlier. I was still grieving. I knew she would have been fascinated by how I was mapping out my life. Widowed with eight children in her early forties, she was an incredibly strong woman who always saw the good in people. I get my strength from her. She loved to travel but didn't get to do much because she wanted to make sure we had a good upbringing. Her life was about putting a roof over our heads, feeding us and clothing us. It was not until later life that she was able to have her own time to explore the world, which she relished.

I soon realised that I couldn't keep going at this pace, going down memory lane with everything I owned, because it would take me a year to pack the flat and I only had around three weeks. I picked up the pace and when I deliberated in my head about something special I took a photograph of it so I still had a memory, then I put it in the bag to go. I packed lots of big bags and deposited them at the charity shops. Much to my amusement, in my last couple of weeks in town I would walk past the same shops seeing items of mine in the window displays. Sometimes I would get a pang of regret and want to rush in and retrieve the item. Mainly I hoped whoever bought it got as much joy out of it as I had done.

I managed to sell most of my furniture. Two of my former work colleagues were moving into a flat and wanted beds. They got mine. I didn't think it through, though, because I had to sleep on my sofa for the last couple of weeks. I just tried to see it as good practice for life in the motorhome. It took a bit of getting used to, though. I would walk into the bedroom then realise I hadn't got a bed and had to make up the sofa. I told myself it was all worth it: no pain, no gain!

Things come together in strange ways. I was struggling to work out how I would dismantle my large sofa and get rid of it when the people moving into my flat contacted me to say they would love to buy many of my bulky items, including the corner sofa, sideboard, wardrobes and my dining table and chairs. I no longer had to worry about lugging those into a van later on, and it added a few more pounds to the coffers.

I had accumulated loads of books over the years because I love reading. They were harder to offload than I had anticipated. I took loads into work and people just chose the ones they wanted. I tried to take lots of them to charity shops but they said they were overloaded with books and refused to take them, so I had to drive round to find shops that would. I was relieved that the more I filled the bags with my possessions, the easier it became. It really did feel like it was lifting a weight from my mind. It is so easy to convince yourself how much you need certain things. Having been on the road now for several years I can assure you that you wouldn't give most of it a second thought, even the few things that you may have put in storage or left with friends to look after. You will realise the value of being able to live in the moment with far less clutter and STUFF and to truly feel happy. It is also nice to wander around shops on your travels knowing that you're not going to buy the souvenirs because you haven't got room in the motorhome and you don't really need those things in your life. They just weigh you down.

Just as I was feeling really stressed by the task ahead of me and that time was running out, I got the most painful ear infection. I called the emergency doctor and ended up in A&E at my local hospital, rocking backwards and forwards because of the pain. I left three hours later with ear drops and very strong antibiotics. For a few days I was in no fit state to focus on sorting through my things. I just felt sorry for myself and took lots of painkillers until the infection subsided. I really didn't know just how painful an ear infection could be until then.

I was also easily distracted by friends inviting me for dinner or out for drinks to say our goodbyes. I soon had only a week to get my act together, which in many ways was good because I just had to get on with it.

There was also the administrative side of creating a different way to live. I needed to change my address on lots of documents, such as my driving licence, passport and insurances. My fab sister-in-law Maggie had agreed to let me use her address as my official address, which was handy. I gave her permission to open all my post and she would then take photographs of anything important, for example vehicle tax renewal notices, and send me the picture.

I made sure I stayed registered with my doctor and dentist. I used the address of a friend to register and then later my daughter's address. This means that I get reminders for mammograms, bowel cancer checks, repeat prescription checks, etc. I can get my HRT prescription sent to a pharmacy nearby when I am travelling and it can be dispensed there. If I need a doctor I can do a phone triage with my doctor or register as a temporary patient at a surgery near where I am staying. The same with my dentist. I schedule regular check-ups when I am back at my daughter's, and if I need emergency treatment on my travels I can find a local dentist for treatment and then visit mine as soon as possible. If I want things delivered to me I can use a click-and-collect service near my campsite. There is always a way around things. As I have found out over the years, you learn things from other people on the road all the time about how to make life as easy as possible.

My boyfriend at the time had agreed to let me store a few things at his house and to stay for two weeks before I hit the road in my motorhome. Seeing the look on his face, I reassured him that it was not me sneakily moving into his house, it was merely me 'transitioning'. I had only been seeing him for about eighteen months, so he was still trying to understand my need to head off in the motorhome, something I had told him I was going to do from the first day I met him. Suffice to say, the relationship fizzled out pretty soon after my alternative lifestyle started. He did meet up with me several times for weekends in the motorhome, but he just couldn't cope with it. I was sad but soon got over it, and to be honest it meant that I put my heart and soul into really finding a different way to live. I had been compromising my trip because I made sure I wasn't too far away for him to visit me. Once I was a free agent I started behaving more freely and it suited me, if I am being truthful. I didn't want to be shackled by what I felt society thought retired pensioners' lives were like: winding down maybe; more sedate; less willing to challenge themselves physically. I wanted to break the rules and push the boundaries in my sixties, to inspire as many women as I could to take opportunities and strive for a fulfilling way of living.

But back to the packing ... I was taking half my things to his and half to Maggie's, in Leeds. The day I moved out of my flat was very stressful. I was quite emotional because I had loved living there for the last ten years. I had ordered a van to be delivered at three o'clock, only to get a phone call from them saying they would deliver a slightly smaller one as they didn't have the size I had ordered and *paid* for. Well, you can imagine, with my stress levels, I hit the roof! After many angry calls to various people I was delivered an enormous white van – far bigger than the one I had ordered. It was all they had left. The kind driver helped me load up my chaise longue and chest of drawers. Then he had to go. I had to use brute force to finish lugging everything else into the vehicle. I was covered in bruises.

Four hours later than planned, I headed off to my boyfriend's: a two-and-a-quarter-hour journey. Oh no! As if my stress levels weren't high enough, I got caught up in an accident on the M25. The queues stretched for miles and we were at a standstill for what seemed like an eternity. A section of motorway was closed for over six hours. I eventually followed a diversion heading for Woking and rejoined the M25 further down. I was exhausted when I eventually arrived at my boyfriend's house in Oxfordshire.

The next morning he helped me unload things into his garage, even though he was still quite confused about what I was doing. Here I was giving up my well-paid, secure job and good home and handing out my worldly possessions to anyone who would take them. I totally get why it was all too much for him to get his head around. Despite his misgivings, he was so helpful. He turned the van around for me because I was too scared to reverse it out of his driveway. I knew I was going to have to get to grips with driving a large vehicle when I got my motorhome in a few weeks, but I would worry about that when I had to. For now I was willing to accept any help on offer.

I planned to head off to Leeds to offload the final remnants of my worldly goods at Maggie's house. First, though, I needed to fill the petrol tank.

I went to the local petrol station where I climbed into the back of the van to get my phone charger. I shut the door behind me, not realising I wouldn't be able to get out again that way because it didn't have an inside handle. I was stuck in the back of the van on the petrol forecourt. I panicked at first, then spotted the side door, blocked by furniture and bags. I struggled for ages moving things around before clambering over all the bags to get out, very dishevelled and sweaty, much to my relief. I had visions of me having to shout and bang on the van sides to get help.

Eventually I arrived in Leeds and deposited the rest of my belongings with Maggie for her to store in her garage. She has always been such a good friend, and even though she too couldn't really get her head around what I was doing, she was excited for me and always so supportive. It is something for which I will be eternally grateful and I thank her from the bottom of my heart. We all need friends like that in our lives. I was just lucky that she also married my brother Jonathan, so she is family too.

Chapter 6

Dora the Explora

The day had finally come for me to pick up my motorhome from Elite Motorhomes in Banbury. I could hardly sleep the night before, realising that my dream of five years or more was becoming a reality. I was going to live in a motorhome and travel around Great Britain for the next year and write about all my experiences, hopefully inspiring other women. Little did I know then that I would actually be on the road for several years and the happiest I have ever been.

When I arrived at the motorhome showroom and saw my low-profile Auto-Trail Tribute 615 sitting there on the forecourt, I knew I had chosen well and couldn't wait to take ownership of it, even though I was about to hand over a hefty cheque for the balance of payment.

When I climbed into it, to my relief it was even nicer than I remembered. I really didn't have a clue what to do with anything. I was very nervous and just hoped I would be able to remember everything they told me. Mercifully one of the sales team gave me a thorough guided tour of the motorhome. He explained exactly how things worked and what I needed to do to ensure they continued to work. He could see my anxious eyes staring back at him as he ran through how the heating system and fridge could run off either the gas cylinders or electricity, if that was available. He suggested I use my phone to video him so that I would have a record of our conversation and something to refer back to if I was confused. I did that, following every instruction and filming every switch with my phone. I was very pleased I did: on many occasions in the coming weeks when I got in a pickle, I had something to refer to to sort out the problem. This applied especially to the clean water tank that needed filling and the dirty water tank that had to be emptied, not to mention the toilet cassette that required emptying and cleaning before adding some special blue chemicals.

After hours of filling out paperwork and getting my instructions, it was time to seal the deal and drive off. He shook my hand and passed me the keys to the motorhome, as well as a black bag full of operating instruction manuals, log books for all parts of the van, various bits of paperwork, guarantees, etc. and the spare keys. I was ready to drive off in my new motorhome, which I had decided to call Dora the Explora.

I climbed up into the cabin and turned the key in the ignition. Normally I love driving, so I just told myself, 'You can do this, don't be scared, take it steady.' I put it into gear, slowly released the clutch and pressed the accelerator … I was off, my journey had begun. My heart beat in my chest. I went goosebumpy and my eyes welled up a bit with the sheer joy and excitement of the moment.

I tentatively drove it back to my boyfriend's house, where I was staying. I could see a line of cars building up behind me as I drove slowly along the road. I had to get used to the dimensions of the vehicle and give myself more space when manoeuvring around roundabouts and country lanes. It meant I was not going very fast at all. Hearing the tree branches brushing over the top of the motorhome on some of the narrower roads was a bit disconcerting, but I got there in one piece. More importantly, so did the motorhome.

Over the next two weeks I cleaned and packed the vehicle for my adventures. It was so difficult trying to decide between what I wanted and what I actually needed on the road trip. At times it felt surreal, as if I was playing house.

I had been having a few nightmares about getting stuck on narrow country roads because the motorhome was too big to navigate them. So I took myself off to Halfords and bought a satnav specifically for motorhomes. You input the vehicle's dimensions and it will only take you on routes where it will fit. This made me feel more confident. I was very pleased with myself because I got £60 off the advertised price in the store. It said, 'We match any price', so I took out my mobile phone and found the same model for £60 less on Amazon, and the salesperson agreed to sell it to me for the lower price. This was the start of the new, more confident me, knowing that I was going to have to live off a tight budget.

The next task was to find some mode of transport to explore places when the motorhome was parked up. Despite not having been on a bike for over forty years, I decided that a bike was the answer. Not any ordinary bike, though: an ebike. I had been reading up a lot about them and realised they were not cheap, but they had great reviews. Off I went again to Halfords. I tested a few bikes around the car park and surrounding roads and finally plumped for the Carrera Crossfire ebike. It has eight gears, but more importantly, when the going gets tough, all I have to do is press a little button to the left of the handlebars and it makes life so much easier up the hills. I couldn't believe how much it made me want to go out cycling. Being impatient, I persuaded the staff at Halfords to sell me the display model; it would fit into the back of my soft-top Mini so that I could take it home there and then. As they approached the car they said, 'It'll never fit, we'll have to take a wheel off', but with a little perseverance and determination and a little help from the long seatbelt, we secured it enough for me to drive off – armed with my shiny new grey and purple cycle helmet. I have to say that no one looks good in a cycle helmet, and I do look particularly bad. But safety first and all that!

I took great delight in inviting people to have a guided tour of the motorhome as it sat on my boyfriend's driveway. His parents, who had been keen caravanners, were so informative and supportive and gave me so many things – chairs, a table, a fab TV – along with lots of sound advice and tips gathered from their many years on campsites.

I had still not spent a night in the motorhome. Elite Motorhomes kindly paid for me to stay on a local campsite. This enabled me to have a little practice at using all parts of the motorhome and making sure I had taken in everything they had told me. I was extremely nervous when I arrived. The first hurdle was to reverse correctly into my pitch. That done, I turned my attention to connecting up the electricity. I unravelled the lead and plugged it into the side of the motorhome and searched for the socket. It took me ages to find it because it was hidden behind a hedge. Next thing to do was switch the gas cylinder on. I was so frightened it would explode if I did something wrong. Because I was so anxious I wasn't able to fathom out which way to turn it for ages and it was very stiff. Then I remembered 'righty tighty, lefty loosey': turn right to close and left to open.

I had cheated with the water, though, as I just didn't want to attempt everything in one go: I got my boyfriend to fill the tank before I left his house. In return I cooked him a lovely salmon stir-fry on my new cooker. He had popped along to check I was okay before I settled down for the night.

If I am honest, I didn't have the best night's sleep in my new surroundings as I was so hyped up by the whole experience. But the following morning I got up and made breakfast with the realisation that I would be okay on the road alone. Yes, I had lots to learn, yes, it would be scary, but I had lots of time to learn it. The most important thing was that I was now the mistress of my own destiny and I loved that feeling – a feeling that I will never tire of.

For the next couple of weeks I set about making sure I had the right equipment for the motorhome and took lots of advice from people who had experienced life on the road in either a caravan or motorhome. I went on lots of social media sites and read about people who had done similar things and learnt what to do and what not to do in certain situations. The more I googled, the more I realised that I would be alright, as there is a wealth of information out there to help you.

There was one person that I needed to see before I became a full-time retirement rebel: Sammy. She was living in London at the time with her boyfriend. I got the train to London and made my way to Putney. We spent a couple of days celebrating her thirty-first birthday. She was just as excited about my future as I was, and we chatted away about how I was going to live and agreed that she and her little dachshund, Frank, would come and stay with me for a few nights as soon as she could get time off work. This would also hopefully allay her fears about what it would be like going from my large flat to a six-metre van. She was concerned about my safety and about me being on my own in the motorhome; venturing into the unknown. Thankfully she is also used to me facing my fears in life as a single mother and coming out the other side. She knows I am made of tough stuff really, and will get wherever it is I am aiming for in the end.

* * *

On 20 September 2019 I drove through the little village on the outskirts of Banbury after telling everyone, 'My plan is to have no plan. I'm going to go with the flow and see where life takes me.' In that moment it felt liberating, not scary at all. The sun was shining and the sky was bright blue with big white fluffy clouds. I just remember feeling so elated that I was facing my fears and actually doing it, not even really knowing what 'it' was, but knowing that it felt so right to be sitting up high in the motorhome, taking in the beauty of my surroundings, driving through the Oxfordshire countryside.

As I made my way tentatively along the country lanes from Banbury to the M40 I have to admit I was shaking. This was the biggest vehicle I had ever driven. I was still getting to grips with its dimensions. My trusted satnav guided me along. I was thrilled that it had such a big screen and I had no problems seeing the maps on it. The voice telling me when to turn left and right was very precise and gave me plenty of notice before junctions, which I very much appreciated. It gave me time to think about positioning the motorhome to take a wider turn than I would have done with my Mini.

Eventually I joined the motorway. I felt as nervous as I did the first time I drove on a motorway after passing my driving test. Now I was dealing with a far larger vehicle and I really had to have my wits about me. Big trucks came up very close behind me, which felt a bit threatening. When they overtook me they were so close and I did feel scared at times. I would slow down and couldn't wait for them to get past. I was acutely aware of how big the motorhome was because as they passed me it was pulled to one side. I had to oversteer to compensate. Eventually I began to get the hang of driving it. I held my own at a steady pace around fifty miles an hour. I then joined the M1 and headed to my brother Paddy's house in Lincolnshire. He is an old hand at this motorhome lark. He was waiting to give me his expert advice and brotherly support, which was much needed. His wife, Lorraine, was going to see how well, or how badly, I had packed things into the lockers. They know all too well the dangers of things falling out when you open lockers after a long drive if the contents aren't stored correctly. I was looking forward to getting her advice.

My brother guided me in as I reversed the vehicle into his driveway. He checked that I had all the right connections and gadgets to make life just that little bit easier. We made a list of other items I needed, such as a thermal screen for the front windows of the cab. Even though I had some screens to put across the windscreen and door windows at night, he said external ones keep the condensation down inside the cab and keep it much warmer. I was up for anything that would keep me warm. We headed off to the local camping shop to buy them under his expert eye. My best purchase was a £15 outdoor gas barbecue.

He also got me to drive to an area of grassland near his house where he showed me a special technique with the clutch to move off soggy grass and not get stuck. Being able to use clutch control to get myself out of tricky situations has been invaluable throughout my time on the road.

I was pleasantly surprised that Lorraine thought I had packed my belongings pretty well for a first attempt. She suggested some slight tweaks but gave me the thumbs-up.

They offered me a nice warm bed in their house, but I was determined to sleep in my van. This was my life now.

The following day my brother guided me through filling up my water tank and checking round the motorhome to make sure everything was packed away before I drove off. It was time to spend a few nights on some campsites in Dora the Explora.

Chapter 7

Getting to Grips with Life on the Road

I had booked a small site not far from Sheffield, near Redmires Reservoirs, so that I didn't have too far to drive from my brother's house. I made sure I would have electricity, as I knew I wasn't ready to try my hand at camping without it in the early days on the road. Baby steps ... I drove on to the site, which was in a field behind a farm, and found my hardstanding spot. The ground was very uneven. It was time to try out my levellers: triangular wedges that you put under the wheels to level out the vehicle with the aid of a spirit level inside the motorhome. Well, it transpired that that was easier said than done for a novice like me. They just kept sliding around as I tried to reverse on to them. Thankfully the couple in the caravan next to me, Keith and Jenny, took pity on me and tried to guide them under the tyres for me. But I was so tired and I kept turning the wheel the wrong way. It was a bit of a disaster. I thanked them for helping and admitted defeat for a while and planned to have a shot at doing it again later when I had calmed down.

I then tried desperately to remember all the things my brother had told me the night before about plugging in the electricity and turning on the gas. I successfully connected myself up to the electricity supply. I did break out into a hot sweat just unravelling the long lead and making sure it wasn't coiled up in places, which I had been told could cause it to overheat and melt. I still struggled to turn on the gas, but eventually I managed it.

I was pretty pleased with the set-up and told myself that I was on a steep learning curve and it would get easier the more I did it. I must not beat myself up or get too stressed because the whole idea of this trip was to just go with the flow and relax. For too long I had been struggling to just get through the day. Now I had the opportunity to start again and hopefully discover a new way of living where I would be true to myself.

I had arranged for Maggie to come down from Leeds and be my first guest so that I had some moral support. We are both in our sixties and ready for a bit of an adventure. It was great to see her friendly face. I have to say I did feel very proud that I had the motorhome all set up with table and chairs outside as if it was something I did all the time. We had a massive hug and giggled at what I was deciding to do with my life. I'm not sure Maggie knew what to make of it all.

It wasn't long before I put her to work helping me get the levellers under the front wheels to straighten out the van. She guided me back perfectly as I drove on to them. There was still a bit of a slant, but we both agreed we could cope with sleeping at a slight angle and it was time to crack open the wine.

I couldn't wait to wow her with my culinary skills on the outside barbecue. I managed to conjure us up spicy chicken, veg and new potatoes. We drank lots of wine and sat under the stars chatting for hours: just what I had dreamt of doing for the last few years.

Making up the beds in the motorhome felt like playing house. We were both excited and it reminded us of when we lived in St James's Hospital in Leeds as part of our nurse training and we used to hang out together with everyone in our small rooms. Just like a childhood sleepover, we chatted until the early hours about how our lives had panned out so far. This made Maggie contemplate when to retire herself.

The next day we got up really early to watch the sunrise. I never stop getting excited seeing the beauty of the sun rising in the sky. Breakfast was bacon butties and mugs of tea. Maggie was as excited as me to be experiencing the novelty of van life. Eventually we headed out on a long walk around Redmires Reservoirs on the stunning moorland. It was quite muddy in places but the scenery was beautiful. We were lucky with the weather: clear blue skies. At one point we took a wrong turn and had to climb over a high wall, which was a challenge for both of us, but we were not going to be stopped in our tracks. As we clambered over I thought to myself, 'There's life in the old dog yet.' I couldn't wait to see what other challenges I would be overcoming in the coming months and years.

Maggie left that evening having thoroughly enjoyed her night in my new home. Time for me to chill out on my own. I enjoyed sitting under the stars again reflecting on just what I had already achieved and what I was planning to do. This was not just a way of living for me: I wanted to show that just because I had retired, it did not mean that I was slowing down and fading into the background. Quite the opposite: I wanted this to be the best part of my life, as well as inspiring women of all ages, particularly other women who are struggling in life like I was; who feel lost and want a sense of purpose and excitement. I wanted to show that when you age you don't become beige and invisible. You can go out there and have a colourful existence. I wanted to get conversations going to mobilise women against ageism and help reframe how we address it, and encourage younger women to implement policies to protect older women in the workplace. For now these were just ideas I was passionate about. I was hoping it would become clearer to me how I would make these changes happen; how I would get my voice heard.

I woke up really early the next day and it was pretty nippy. I was surprised just how well I had slept after struggling to get to sleep on my own. I was still coming to terms with the fact that this was my home and this was my future life. I jumped out of bed, threw on my dressing gown and slippers and, feeling very bleary-eyed, opened the door of the motorhome. Looking out across the farm fields and countryside, I had a childlike feeling of excitement in my stomach. There was no one else in the field, so I ran around in my slippers in the morning dew that had settled on the grass around me. In the distance I could see the sun peeking out from the horizon. The day was beginning and I was excited about the uncertainty of what it would bring. I also realised that I needed to get myself some waterproof boots to slip on if this was going to be my morning routine, as my slippers and feet quickly became drenched.

For years, as a news presenter, reporter and producer at the BBC, there had been so many deadlines and pressures to get news stories to air on time. My life was governed by a rota system. I had someone else deciding what days and hours I worked, often changing my shift patterns at the last minute, which I always found very stressful, being a single mother. I couldn't plan things in advance and when I did, I then had to change my plans to accommodate the work rotas. Now here I was deciding in my sixties to let my life be all about not having a plan, going with the flow and just seeing where things took me. I was literally stepping into the unknown. As I watched the sun slowly rising on that misty September morning in Yorkshire, I knew in my heart that I was doing the right thing. I had quit my job at sixty, announcing that I would get rid of my flat and most of my possessions to live in a motorhome and travel around Great Britain. I was saying that I didn't need all that STUFF any more to make me happy. In fact, I was going as far as saying I would be even happier without it all. This amused so many of my family and friends because they just could not see me settling into life on the road. I was the person who liked the finer things in life, and enjoyed popping open the champagne when they came to visit. I hosted lots of dinner parties and enjoyed having people around me and in my home all the time. Now here I was going off on my own, to who knows where. How on earth would I cope with having to empty my own loo every day? Lug cans of water across a field to fill up the water tank? Drive a big motorhome all around the country on my own?

Surprisingly, this morning I did not feel cold as I watched the sun slowly rising, I think probably because I was too excited to feel that chill. I loved that I was allowing myself to take in the moment and to enjoy the sensations of freedom, fear, excitement and wonder.

When I turned around to go back and make my early morning cup of coffee, I noticed just how much the van was tilting to one side, even with the levellers under the wheels. It made me giggle to myself, although I was pleased with what I had done to settle into the site and felt that sleeping a little bit wonky was acceptable. I would work out the levellers another day. I kept chuckling to myself, enjoying the uncertainty of what I would do next.

A few hours later I got some neighbours on the farm. I have to say I was in awe of them straight away. I sat in my motorhome staring out of the window to see if I could learn a thing or two. They pulled up and were a prime example of how to set up your motorhome in record time. It seemed like he had his jobs outside and she had hers inside, like a well-oiled machine. I could only aspire to be like them one day. Until then I would watch and rewatch the videos I made when I picked up the motorhome, with the salesman telling me what I needed to do to connect things and what buttons to press to switch on the water pump, heat the water, etc.

Still eager to learn from the couple, I got my table and chair out of the van and positioned them so that I would catch their eye as they walked past. We soon got chatting and they were so lovely and remembered clearly how they had felt when they first took to the road a couple of years before. They reassured me that things would get better and I would learn so much. They passed on lots of tips and showed me various kitchen gadgets to make motorhome cooking much easier. I took photographs of the items which I hoped to purchase in due course. They even showed me how to put my levellers in properly so that I would have a more even night's sleep.

I had my housekeeping jobs to do, which included emptying the loo. Most sites have a special chemical point to empty them into. It didn't faze me, to be honest: when I was nursing I emptied hundreds of bedpans. This was a cassette, like a small suitcase, with a funnel that was easy to empty and rinse out. I also needed to fill my water tank up a bit more. I was still confused about how to attach the hosepipe to the tap fitting. Instead I went back and forth with my little watering can to fill it. My neighbours watched from afar, bemused. I told myself it was okay because it was also good exercise for me. I had all the time in the world to do it, and I was happy. The views over the hills of the cattle and sheep were an added bonus. I would get to grips with that hosepipe another day.

I was glad these had been my first neighbours because it just reaffirmed what I wanted to experience on my travels: meeting kind, friendly people who restore one's faith in human nature. I had spent far too much of my life being treated in a way that was not acceptable, partly because I feared speaking up for myself. It felt so empowering to know that I never had to do that again. Now I could be who I really was and show kindness and friendship to people along the way and learn from them. It was such a release. It felt good to be in that place, although I knew I had only begun to unleash the me that had been struggling to get out for many years.

When I packed up to move on to the next site that I had booked through the Caravan and Motorhome Club, I went through my checklist: checking that the skylights were closed, the gas was switched off and everything was packed securely into the lockers so it wouldn't fall out; ensuring the toilet and dirty-water tank were emptied. Thinking that all was shipshape, I climbed into the driver's seat to head off. Panic set in: I had almost driven off with the levellers still in place. Fortunately I remembered at the last second and stopped myself. I drove off them and clambered back out to pack them away.

Having experienced the smaller, intimate farm site it was a bit of a shock to see so many motorhomes and caravans so close together at my next site in Castleton in the Peak District. It was a lot more formal. I felt overwhelmed. I got a warm greeting from the warden, who explained how to follow the one-way system, choose a pitch and park up. I told her that I was very new to life on the road. She encouraged me to venture out and explore the area and showed me lots of maps and routes, reassuring me that I would get to grips with all the filling and emptying of water. I struggled to understand the one-way system and find my pitch. I could choose any empty pitch with a white post. The trouble was I needed long-distance glasses to see where I was driving and my short-distance glasses to read the one-way map. So I was constantly swapping my glasses and getting more and more stressed. Eventually I found a spot and parked up, only to be told by the warden fifteen minutes later that I had to move it over and line it up with the white post to keep a safe fire distance. It would take a long time before I stopped getting het up on the larger sites.

There was something nice about having shower blocks, laundry and washing-up facilities on the larger sites, so they were good for a few days to get my washing done as I got accustomed to my new way of life. But they were a bit soulless for me. I wanted to get back on to the small sites, back into nature.

I was thrilled that a friend I had worked with in a TV newsroom was working down the road at BBC Radio Sheffield. She came to visit me on site. When she phoned I was exploring Castleton and I hurried back to make my home presentable for her. I was happy to welcome another guest into my home and couldn't wait to show it off. We spent a few hours catching up on the latest gossip and I cooked us a spicy stir-fry, with strawberries for dessert. When she left I sat and watched the sun setting, feeling a warm glow that life was good and it was only going to get better.

The following day I got up early, packed a drink and some snacks and headed off to discover Hope, about a mile and a half down the road. It was very pretty, surrounded by hills. Wanting to economise now that I was living off a pension, I walked back to the motorhome, made myself a sandwich and headed out again on my ebike. That was after struggling for ages to lift it down from the bike stand. I was going to have to practise to find a better technique. It was a bit heavier than I thought it would be and I needed to build up my arm muscles.

Later, I cycled back from Hope, through Brough and beyond. The whole area was breathtakingly beautiful. I could have burst with happiness tootling along on the bike and taking in my surroundings.

It was time to really test out the ebike on a one-in-twenty incline on the hill to some scenic caves. The battery didn't let me down. It kicked in and I managed to pedal three quarters of the way up. People turned around in their cars to look, as if to say, 'How the heck is she getting up this hill so easily when even some cars are struggling?', which made me laugh. I just kept pedalling like mad trying to make it look like I was doing most of the work and I was just superfit – which was far from the truth. Eventually it was too steep for me to keep pedalling and I admitted defeat. Feeling tired by this time, I turned the bike round and headed home. It was a bit scary going down the steep hill. I had this dialogue going on in my head saying,

'What would happen if I pulled the brakes too hard? Would I go flying over the handlebars?' Thankfully I managed to hold it together and got down safely.

When I got back to the site, exhausted after my cycle ride, I struggled to get the bike on the bike rack. It must have been very entertaining for the people in the surrounding caravans and motorhomes watching me through their windows. I prayed they weren't laughing at me.

As I sat with my feet up and a gin and tonic that evening in Dora the Explora, I felt a great sense of achievement with the day's activities: a couple of hours' walk and a two-hour bike ride. I have to admit I did have a little power nap when I got back, which I loved. It was wonderful to just be able to do what I wanted, when I wanted.

Full of the joys of the day, I went over to the shower block to have a well-earned shower. When I got back I got a call from a radio producer at BBC Radio Sheffield. My friend had told them what I was doing and they were intrigued. They wanted to interview me about my life on the road as a retirement rebel. Could I kindly drive my motorhome to the studio later that week? I was so excited. Here was a chance for me to get out my message about positive ageing. Hopefully this was the start of me connecting with and inspiring more women. I knew Rony Robinson, the presenter, from when I had worked at BBC Radio Sheffield for a year when Sammy was very small, so it would be great to be interviewed by him.

Feeling elated, I set to making myself a dinner of salmon fillet, veg and new potatoes. I was loving creating healthy meals in my kitchen area, just as I had done in my large flat. As I reached for my outdoor jacket to take the pots and pans to the washing-up sinks, I realised it wasn't there. My heart sank. I had left my expensive waterproof jacket hanging on the door inside the shower cubicle. I felt sick because I knew that it was vital for my motorhome living and I couldn't afford to replace it if it was gone. I rushed to the shower block and it was nowhere to be seen. I just hoped that some kind soul had handed it in to the wardens on the site. I had a long overnight wait to find out. I would be gutted if they hadn't.

I got up really early and stood outside the office waiting for it to open. The moment they unlocked the door I shot in and asked if anyone had handed it in. Sadly they had not. I just felt awful all day. I had assumed that in these kinds of places there would be a sense of togetherness and honesty; that people in motorhomes and campervans would look out for one another.

Just as I was feeling really sorry for myself in the afternoon there was a knock on my door. The warden stood there smiling with my purple jacket in her hand. Someone had had a lazy morning so they hadn't got around to handing it in until after lunch.

My mood completely changed. I was thrilled, because I hadn't wanted to think someone would have taken it, knowing it wasn't theirs. All was good with the world.

* * *

I was still familiarising myself with the various types of campsite I could book. There are 'certified locations' affiliated to the Caravan and Motorhome Club, which take five units of motorhomes and caravans. Then there are 'certified sites' affiliated to the Camping and Caravanning Club, which allow five units plus a few tents. Both organisations also have their club sites that offer discounts for the over-sixties in some cases. At the time I wasn't focusing on where I would travel to, rather how I was getting on with changing my lifestyle completely. I was learning to live in a small space with far less stuff; working out how best I wanted to do things. For example, I had to decide whether to leave a bed made up all the time and just cover it with a throw during the day so I could use it as a seat or put the bed away every morning. I prefer the second option. Currently I wake up, put the kettle on, make a cup of coffee and switch the water heater on so that I can have a shower, if I don't use the communal facilities on a site. Then I pack my bedding and bed away. If I want a lazy morning, I just pull one of my rugs over me and relax with a cup of coffee. I think the temptation to lounge all day on the bed would be too much for me if I left it made up.

I realised too that the types of places I stay in make me feel differently about what I am doing. At the moment I seem to favour the smaller locations in rural settings. I don't know if that will change as I go along. I am going to keep on sampling all types of camping facilities to fine-tune my likes and dislikes. I am writing blogs on *shuvonshuvoff.blogspot.com* as I go along so that eventually I can look back and see just how far I have come.

My next port of call was Chatsworth Park campsite. I was still extremely nervous about driving around in the motorhome, getting to grips with the width of the road and just how fast to go. I tried not to feel pressured by the cars behind me to go faster than I was comfortable with. If I am honest, it did stress me out a bit. At one stage, when I was struggling to find the campsite, I pulled over into a lay-by. I got a KitKat from the cupboard and a cup of water and took five minutes to calm down and regroup. Then I set off again to find the site. It was such a relief to be able to do that in my little house on wheels.

It was another large site with many caravans and motorhomes. At least this time they were nicely spaced out. I wasn't feeling it, but it was good to have the laundry facilities and I took advantage of them and did a lot of washing. This also saved my water and meant I still did not have to fill my water tank, a task that I knew was looming, and I would have to fathom out a way to fill it with the hosepipe. I couldn't fill it with watering cans forever.

When I checked into the site, they gave me a key which allowed me to go through into the grounds of Chatsworth House and walk around as much as I liked. I found the door in the wall, which reminded me of one of my favourite books as a child, *The Secret Garden*, and I unlocked it and prised it open. I was blown away with just how beautiful the grounds were, and the icing on the cake was a massive rainbow above the house. I walked for miles exploring. Luckily I timed it during a break in some heavy rainstorms. The beauty of my surroundings made me tearful. I felt so happy that I had the time to stop and take in the moment. I began to realise that this trip was going to be magical. The rainbow being there when I came through the gate was a sign for me. Rainbows are special and make me feel that I can do anything and I am heading in the right direction with my life. And don't get me started on what I am like if I see a double rainbow!

The next day there was no let-up in the rain, but I was not going to let that deter me from doing a six-mile walk over Parkhouse Hill, north of the River Dove, and over Chrome Hill.

It was a bit tricky in parts because of the heavy rain and strong winds, but well worth it for the incredible views. As if that wasn't enough, I also tackled Hollins Hill, which is 450 metres high. Thankfully the rain held off during that section and I managed to dry off a bit. I held my breath along the narrow section in the high winds. At times I did wonder why the heck I was walking in such bad weather. It was tough going, but I did have a great sense of achievement when I finished, even if I was sodden.

It was finally time to address the elephant in the room: filling my water tank with a hosepipe. I knew that I was moving on to a more remote site where it might not be as easy to access water.

I struggled for what seemed like an eternity just to get the water cap off in the rain. It would not budge. I could feel the eyes of the other campers piercing my back. I imagined them commenting on how useless I was. One fellow camper eventually took pity on me and kindly came out in the rain to show me how to open it and attach the hosepipe. Hooray! I finally filled the water tank myself. To me that was a major milestone.

Not before time, as I had to be at BBC Radio Sheffield for an interview with Rony Robinson. It was the first time I had driven through a busy city. The route to the studio was very hilly. I had to do lots of hill starts using my handbrake, which is difficult because it takes a lot of energy to use and is low down on the right-hand side of the driver's seat. It is counterintuitive after years of using my left hand in a conventional car. I presume it is on the right to stop people knocking it getting in and out of the driving seats from the main living area. I was pleased I got there in one piece, if a bit frazzled.

I parked up and Rony interviewed me outside the studio. He loved seeing inside my motorhome. He was fascinated to see where I had the loo and how I emptied it, a question everyone seems to ask me. I showed him how I packed up all my stuff, which he found incredible. I was living with so few possessions. I assured him that I had everything I wanted in life in the motorhome. I stressed that it was very early days and I was most certainly on a sharp learning curve; that I had my tearful moments of frustration. I even recounted my disastrous attempt to fill the water tank myself, much to his amusement. I said I was lucky I could take my time and learn from my mistakes and hopefully I would become an expert by the end of my adventure, however long that would be.

The next thing to overcome was getting out of the radio station car park. It was packed with vehicles. I took the bull by the horns and did a three-point turn. I was so pleased with myself. And I headed off to my next destination in Harrogate.

Chapter 8
Best Friends' Trip

Who better to help me continue my journey up north than two of my best friends, Ann and Maggie? I have known them since I was eighteen, when we all started our nurse training at St James's Hospital in Leeds in 1977. Maggie got together with my brother Jonathan at a nurses' house party. The three of us are over sixty now and our lives have taken different paths. Ann returned to Cork after she finished her training; she married and had five children, while continuing to nurse. I ventured into journalism and Maggie worked as a practice nurse for many years. Our friendships have endured many ups and downs through the years. We have always been there to celebrate the good times and support each other through the bad, although we all agree that we are pretty useless at keeping in regular contact. When we do reconnect we have such a great time we ask ourselves why we don't do it more often.

It was an obvious choice for me to have them alongside me in the motorhome in the county where I was born. Even though I have not lived there for many years, you can never take Yorkshire out of my heart and soul.

I picked Maggie up from her house in Leeds. We had supported each other through Jonathan's death, and now she wanted to be a support to me on what I hoped was going to be a life-changing trip. She eagerly jumped aboard Dora the Explora. Ann flew in from Cork and we picked her up at Leeds Bradford Airport. As soon as she came through arrivals we all squealed and hugged one another. People stopped and stared because we caused such a commotion. We are always transported back to the years we lived together in the nurses' home and all the trips to Europe we took together in our twenties.

We were like giggling schoolgirls clambering into the motorhome and putting away the bags, before we set off to our first destination at Pool Bank Farm, not too far from Otley. I was still very tentative about manoeuvring the motorhome, getting to grips with the height and width of it as I drove along past hedgerows and overhanging trees. I very much wanted to impress Ann and Maggie, so I focused all my attention on doing a good job. The entrance to the campsite was very steep and my heart was in my mouth as I chose a gear and willed the motorhome to make it slowly to the top of the hill and round the bend to where we finally stopped. I reversed back into our space and marvelled at the view over Wharfedale. The girls helped me get the table and chairs out as I connected us to the electricity supply and filled the water tank. I was far more proficient because I had managed to practise doing it a few times beforehand. I think they were suitably impressed with my efforts, although I think I did annoy them a bit by stressing about taking our boots off before getting into the motorhome. I knew I was going to have to work on not getting het up when I had guests because I wanted to be welcoming and not stress them out with 'house rules' (I am a work in progress on that front). I decided that one solution would be to buy a mat to put by the steps and a big box to put the boots in. These girls know me so well and can soon put me in my place, which always makes us laugh. I knew they would be great as some of my first guests precisely because they wouldn't take any nonsense from me and would let me know what works and what doesn't, being in such a confined space together.

I made us a delicious dinner, and we wrapped up warm under blankets and sat outside to eat it. We enjoyed the view over Wharfedale and spent the night drinking gin and chatting about what we had been up to. I can highly recommend Dingle Gin, which Ann brought over with her from Ireland. That went down a treat.

They were fascinated that I had got rid of most of my possessions and my flat to live this life and they wanted to know more about it. They both said they could never do it, but they were envious of my decision and intrigued to see where my path took me and if I would be able to find that place in my life I was hoping to find. One thing is certain: anything would be better than the way I had been living. I was just existing and pretending for the last few years at work. I was feeling more and more broken. This was my escape route. The route to where ... was yet to be determined, but it was exhilarating having that uncertainty ahead of me and knowing I was the one who would now be able to determine what I did and didn't do.

I explained how I wanted to challenge ageism in a society that is very ageist. This led us on to talking about how we feel about getting older and what being old means to us. We all agreed that the narratives surrounding ageing need to change. We want people to talk about being pro-age and to stop society's obsession with having to look or feel younger than you are; to be seen to look good. Old is good. We love having the chance to age. Having been nurses we know all too well that life is precious; too many do not get the opportunity to age at all. We also agreed that the media and advertising do not reflect how we age now. They continue to perpetuate negative and pessimistic images, instead of showing better, more energetic lives and positive ways to age. I explained that I wanted to be a role model for women who feel they want more fun in their retirement, and to show them that they can age differently.

It was wonderful to have this kind of discussion with them because I truly want to help women navigate their fears about getting older; to help them speak up for themselves when facing ageism, especially in the workplace; to help them live their best lives and have adventures, no matter how big or small. I want to lead by example.

I was still unsure exactly how I was going to get that message out or what my motorhome madness would turn out to be, but I had a gut feeling that somehow I would work out a way to connect with women and help them feel better about them-selves and inspire them.

* * *

We bunkered down for the night in the bed which spanned the full width of the motorhome. It took us a while to settle because we kept giggling. The laughter continued in the morning when I opened the overhead cupboard and managed to cover Maggie in All-Bran because I hadn't packed the tub properly, leaving her in total shock.

The girls were impressed that there was enough water in the tank for us all to have a hot shower. We had a lovely walk to Otley Chevin. At one point we went off track and wandered into a field where we slowly realised there was a massive bull sitting down in the distance, just looking in our direction. I have never walked up a hill so fast in my life and was extremely relieved when we found a fairly low wall. We all hurriedly clambered over it laughing with relief. We were glad to grab a drink and some lunch in Otley afterwards. The town is very pretty, full of historic buildings and cobbled market areas.

We drove to the Lake District, navigating some pretty narrow roads. The hedgerows scratched at the side of the van, which was a sound I had to get used to because I had no alternative if I was to drive along these types of roads. I was glad to have the girls with me to guide me and to give me the courage to carry on. This was our joint adventure and we were in it together. To me this is what being old is all about: facing your fears and overcoming them bit by bit. It is even better if you have the support of your good mates.

After only a couple of days we had got into sync so that we were able to set up the motorhome on the site very quickly. We all mucked in, one getting the water, another connecting the electricity lead and another turning on the gas supply. Before we knew it we were all sorted. We did intend to do a long walk, but after a mile or so we came across a wonderful pub called the Drunken Duck Inn, with some fantastic brews and views to die for. Needless to say there was not much walking done on day one. We relaxed at the pub, had a few beers and had lots of good old belly laughs recounting life back when we were nurses and how we thought our lives would pan out – and how they actually have panned out.

That night it was Maggie's turn to provide the gin as we played cards … It was called Gunpowder Gin. I don't know what is in it but after a few glasses we all had a very good night's sleep.

It was lovely to sit around and enjoy a lazy breakfast in bed. Ann and I talked about how we were enjoying early retirement. (Maggie does not plan to retire for another couple of years yet.) Ann loves the fact that she has more time to spend with her grandchildren. She also likes the freedom she has not working night shifts any more. I never knew how she did them for so many years, but it was the only way she could juggle being a mother and working.

We remembered that when we started nursing in 1977 people who were sixty were already classed as geriatric patients. Many went into nursing homes at that age, and here we were planning our next adventures.

As if to prove that we are up for a challenge in our sixties, we headed off to Skelwith Fold, where we started our walk to climb Loughrigg Fell in the Central Lakes. At 335 metres high it stands at the end of the ridge coming down from High Raise over Silver How, towards Ambleside.

Maggie had done the route before so we followed her, but we weren't totally sure of our direction so stopped to ask someone with a map. They confirmed we were heading in the right direction. Eventually we were treated to some spectacular views from the top, where there were very few people. On our way back down it was very busy with lots of Saturday day trippers making their way to the summit.

As we ate our last breakfast together in Dora the Explora, I glanced across at my friends and realised how lucky I was to spend such quality time with them. Before I retired, being a busy, working single mother, I had not always felt up to hanging out with friends, and often when I did I was just going through the motions because I was so tired. I think many of us find ourselves in the trap of too much work and not enough play.

Over the last few days we had felt like the women who started nursing together and lived in the nurses' home all those years ago. We were embracing being old and loving life, but it was nice to reflect on times gone by.

We packed up the motorhome. I knew now that I needed to take the grill pan out of the cooker and wedge it under a blanket, and the glass tray from the microwave, so that they didn't rattle when I was driving. I checked that the skylights were firmly shut so they didn't fly off as I was going on my merry way along the country roads. I turned off the gas cylinder and emptied the grey water tank so it didn't slosh around when I was on the road. Most importantly, I made sure that things were securely packed away in the cupboards so that they didn't tumble out.

My driving skills were soon challenged as we headed into Ambleside. There was a very steep junction, just as we headed towards the car park. I struggled with the handbrake and panicked a little. I was fortunate to have the girls with me as they kept me calm. Ann encouraged me by saying, 'You can do this.' I slowly inched the motorhome over the top of the hill and made it into the car park. It did shake me a little and reaffirmed to me that I still had some way to go before I felt truly comfortable driving the motorhome.

As if that wasn't enough, I then struggled to line up the motorhome in the designated space. The parking slots were at such an odd angle. I was back and forth and back and forth for ages before I finally settled on my parking position. The girls just sat quietly and let me get on with it.

I think we were all so pleased that we had made it in one piece that we got a bit giggly as we wandered along the shore of Windermere.

We missed the boat trip because we spent too long in a shop, so we decided to grab some fish and chips. Both Ann and Maggie wanted to pay for them, each urging the man behind the counter to take their cash cards for payment. This amused him and eventually he took both, shuffled them and picked a winner. Ann won and Maggie was not happy. She said she was going home. A small crowd had gathered to watch what was happening because we were making such a commotion. They thought it was very entertaining and wanted to see who would eventually pay the bill. I videoed the whole thing and later that day we just fell about laughing watching it play out on the screen.

Our time in the motorhome had come to an end. We had had a blast reconnecting and going over old times and updating each other with what our lives were like now. Where had all the years gone? Their unwavering support throughout my life has meant a lot to me, and seeing that they are 100 per cent behind my lifestyle makes me feel stronger and more resolute to continue on my path to happiness. Sammy calls me the Happiness Chaser.

Chapter 9

Mother and Daughter: Time to Pause and Reflect

I know that heading off on the road in my motorhome will seem selfish to some people. It is, and I make no bones about that. It is something I knew I needed to do to find myself. For so many years I had thrown myself into work while also being a single mother, like so many other women. Then I found myself having the 'what now?' moment: 'What is my life about?' 'What's the next phase of my life going to be like?' I had a strong desire to be heard and not to feel invisible as I got older, especially after struggling with the menopause and feeling browbeaten at work. I didn't want to carry on facing the world with a smile while inside I was crying, a situation that many women who write to me say they struggle with. They too want to find a solution to their unhappiness in later life. They want some excitement, something that will challenge them and make them feel alive, rather than just existing. They want to come out a new person, and stronger.

What I now realise I didn't take into account was Sammy's reaction to me getting rid of my home and possessions and downsizing to a motorhome. We have a close but sometimes challenging relationship, as we are both strong-minded. We have been through a lot in our lives together.

Looking back, I accept that she shouldered a lot in her childhood because she had to grow up pretty quickly and be independent. I was constantly trying to better my career, to earn money, to live in nicer places, so that she would have the opportunity to go to good schools. That's all well and good, but I didn't factor in the impact all my moving around would have on her. I feel sad that I didn't know that then.

She had to repeatedly settle into new schools and make new friends. She was always the new person in a well-established group of friends. In the meantime I was working long hours, which often meant that she had to fend for herself at an early age. It is an awful lot to ask of a child. She never showed me that it made her sad or unhappy. Quite the opposite, she was the best daughter a mother could wish for: she did well in school, played the piano and did lots of extra classes like drama and singing lessons; she would make me laugh so much sometimes that my belly ached. She was my little buddy and I loved hanging out with her.

My excitement was palpable as I waited for her and her little dog Frank to get off the train at Derby so that we could have our motorhome adventure together. I wanted her to experience my sense of freedom and happiness. It was important to me that she was happy with what I was doing. Being together in the motorhome would give us the opportunity to relax together and to have conversations about life in general, without the pressures of work. My life before I took to the road had been a constant rush to get things done, not always achieving my goal.

Being exhausted and so full of anger I could not sit still and see the wood for the trees.

It was time for me to pause, to reflect on Sammy's and my experiences together; to listen to her; to find out how she saw things. Unless I stopped and took time to reflect and put things into context, how would I know what my life meant? How would I know what to change to make life better for me and for Sammy, if necessary? I was extending and challenging myself to think about life differently, and this was all part of the process.

I was staying about a twenty-minute drive away in a field on the outskirts of the pretty Derbyshire village of Tissington. There is a fine Jacobean manor which has been home to the FitzHerbert family for over 400 years. There is an old-fashioned sweet shop – unfortunately for me it was closed – and a lovely candle-making shop. I knew that Sammy would love wandering around the quaint place.

I was fascinated to learn that Tissington has an extra-special well-dressing ceremony. I had never heard of anything like it. No one seems to know exactly why the five wells started to be dressed every year, but one theory is that it began just after the Black Death of 1348. The population round about was ravaged by the plague, but Tissington was not affected and they think that was because the water was so pure. Ever since then the wells have been decorated around Ascension Day, and the clergy go around and bless them – something of interest with which to regale Sammy when she arrived.

I saw Sammy's bright yellow raincoat in the distance and noticed that Frank was sporting a similar one, which made me laugh. There were lots of squeals and hugs before I bundled them into the motorhome and we headed off to the site.

Straight away Sammy loved being in the passenger seat so high up. She got a far better view of the countryside as I drove along.

From the very beginning Sammy had supported me in our conversations when I was planning to head off in September 2019, although it must have been hard for her to get her head around what I was doing because I kept saying, 'I don't really know where I'll be going or what I'll be doing. I'll see where life takes me. I do know that I'll be challenging ageist attitudes and hopefully inspiring women to age more positively.'

Now she was going to experience a bit of the unknown in Dora the Explora, and I wasn't sure what she would think of it all after her stay. I admit to feeling a bit apprehensive.

She loved that I was the only motorhome in the field and that it was so picturesque. It was such a lovely day – we just threw her bag into the van then went for a walk along the Tissington Trail, a former railway line which is now a bridleway, cycleway and footpath. We walked all the way to Ashbourne and back, chatting non-stop. Frank was so happy to stretch his little legs after the long train journey.

From the moment they stepped foot in the motorhome they were at home. Frank was just big enough to put his paws on the back of the seat to perch himself up so that he could look out of the window. He was on guard all the time, barking at passing horses or cows in the next field. He wasn't going to let anyone get to us. I had not really been a dog person before she got Frank, but now I absolutely adore him and love being his 'grandpawrent'. I am always asking Sammy to send me videos of him being mischievous.

We wrapped up warm and rolled out the awning at the side of the motorhome and sat outside with nibbles and a gin and tonic to continue having a good old natter and catch-up. I was thrilled that Sammy liked the motorhome so much. It was far more spacious and homely than she had envisaged. She said, 'I get it, Mum, I could live in a place like this.'

After dinner we made up the bed across the full width of the motorhome so that there was plenty of room for us and Frank in the middle. I loved having our girlie sleepover. We kept making each other laugh, recounting events from her childhood, before we eventually dropped off to sleep.

We jumped out of bed very early the next day, pulled on our wellies, threw open the door of the motorhome and stepped outside to watch the spectacular sunrise. The morning dew was visible in the dawn light. We didn't care that we were in our pyjamas. That just added to the excitement and sense of freedom that we both experienced. It was wonderful being so carefree, Sammy in her thirties and me in my sixties. We were transported back to when she was a little girl and we would go camping in our little two-man tent and do crazy things like this all the time. We didn't feel the cold; we just kept laughing and giggling. I felt so happy and so alive. These were the moments that I had not had time for because my life had been so stressful. Now I would cherish this moment forever.

Sammy volunteered to help me with my daily tasks. I was lucky that she liked the novelty of refilling the water tank from the tap at the other side of the field. Shame she wasn't interested in emptying the toilet cassette! Frank was loving the freedom of running around the big field. I was so impressed that every time he had to get back into the motorhome, he waited patiently to be cleaned and dried with a towel, before bounding inside.

One day we wandered down into Tissington village and had afternoon tea together in the charming tea shop. It was nice to treat ourselves to a bit of luxury after economising in my van life. There is something special about having afternoon tea with your daughter. It was nice to feel that we could still have the same kind of girlie catch-ups, even though we'll never know where in the country that reunion will be.

Soon our time together was drawing to a close. The days had passed too quickly. As we drove to the station, Sammy told me just how much she had enjoyed chilling with me in the motorhome. She said it was great for her to see what kind of life I was creating for myself and hoped that it became what I was looking for. She vowed to not leave it too long before they joined me again on the road. I dropped them off at the train station. I couldn't help crying as I waved them off.

Driving back to the campsite, past the rolling Peak District hills and farmland, I smiled to myself because I felt our time together had brought us even closer. I felt that I had found a better sense of inner peace.

It was good to hear from Sammy what she thought about things. Yes, she would worry about where I was and what I was doing, but she would do that anyway if I lived in a house, because that's the caring daughter she is.

My journey in the motorhome has been mental as well as physical. I have experienced inner turmoil about what could be expected of me as a mother and people's expectations of what a mother would or should do. Was it okay to just take myself off? Well, having talked to Sammy, the answer is irrevocably yes. There will be women out there who cannot necessarily do that, but they may well be able to find some me time; carve out some place in their life to have an adventure. The important thing is to talk things through with loved ones; outline why you have a desire to do something and try to work out ways together that you can achieve your goals. I know that so many of the decisions I made were a lot easier because I didn't have to consider my actions on others, apart from Sammy.

If I am honest, once I got the idea to get rid of my home and possessions I just ran with it because I knew I needed to do it. Somehow it all made sense to me that that was the way I would truly be happy. I no longer wanted to compromise or pretend in life.

If I was ever in any doubt where I stood in my relationship with my daughter, after spending these years on the road in my van, what she posted on social media for me on Mother's Day recently gave me my answer:

'On Mother's Day I usually post pictures of us together. Today I haven't – because honestly, I can't pin her down long enough to get a recent one!

It has been an incredibly inspiring realisation that I don't actually have to worry about my mum. Anyone in their thirties+ will know, the balance between parent and child shifts, it just does. All you can ask is that your parents live the best life they can and pray they never need you for physical care and support.

Jesus Christ, the last time I panicked that I hadn't heard from my mum in three days, I finally knew she was alright because she posted a picture of her IN THE SEA in the Outer Hebrides.

Look, I love you. You're bonkers. You're inspiring.

You're the Eddie to my Saffy. Your future is incredible.
You're a badass. You're everything. I am motivated by you.
Daily. Actually 'Shuvit' – we all are. You're a crazy bitch …
and I think I might be too.'

When I read it, it filled my heart with joy. She really does get it!
She is a chip off the old block and we can both continue to get
old in our own unique ways, knowing that life is for living and
loving and that there is no one size fits all. We have to find out
what makes us the best version of ourselves. I am so proud of
her and love her very much. I cannot wait for her to join me on
the road again so that we can have more adventures together.

Chapter 10
Loch Morlich:
My Life-Changing Moment

Even though I was settling into and enjoying my life in the motorhome, there was the elephant in the room that I knew I could not just run away from: my state of mind. I had never faced up to deaths in my family: my father when I was sixteen, both my older brother and sister from lung cancer at the age of fifty-three, and my mother ten months previously. I really missed her. Added to these were all the emotional experiences that had prompted me to make this lifestyle change in the first place, and to help other women not feel as desperate as I had.

I was still full of anger about how my life had panned out in my mid- to late fifties. That feeling of being invisible and voiceless in work had a massive impact on how I felt about myself. It eroded my confidence in other aspects of my life. I had an internal dialogue in my head, even questioning if people really liked me, or if my opinion was worth listening to, a far cry from the woman who ran over the finish line in the Brighton Marathon with such confidence about how she would move forward. I knew from speaking to lots of women that they have had similar experiences when their children have grown up and left home or gone off to uni; you start to question what you are doing with your life. You realise that you don't really feel passionate about anything. You just feel beaten down by what life has to offer. You feel that somehow it is too late to start having adventures and doing something new.

That is precisely why I was not going to settle for what life was offering me. I was going to go out there and make my life what I wanted it to be; put my money where my mouth was; show other women that they too could find their passion in life again. I was no longer going to pretend that things were okay, because that had made me feel physically poorly. At one point I hit rock bottom and just wanted to curl up and sleep all the time. I am so glad now that I didn't, because I would have missed what has become the best phase of my life. I want my story to be relatable to women because I have experienced so many of the same things they have: struggling as a single mother working full time; having a hysterectomy; bereavement; feeling invisible, voiceless and marginalised in the workplace by ageist attitudes when I was also struggling with the menopause.

With all this in mind, I headed off to Scotland in Dora the Explora in January 2020. I hadn't been north of the border for many years, but I knew I loved it. Often when I had had particularly bad days at work, I would say to my colleagues, 'I just feel like running off to a loch in Scotland and screaming at the top of my voice.'

The more I thought about it, the more it seemed like a bloomin' good idea. I did my research and eventually settled on one loch that I liked the look of: Loch Morlich near Aviemore.

As I drove into Scotland and saw the Scottish flag sign on the side of the road I felt a warmth inside me, as if I knew that somehow this was the place where I would be able to sort my mind out. The weather was crazy along the route: one moment the clouds were so low I had to drive through them, then around the corner there was a bright blue sky. Heading past Kingussie, I felt quite emotional as I looked across to the beautiful snow-capped hills in the distance.

After a very long drive I was relieved to eventually pull into the Glenmore Camping in the Forest site alongside Loch Morlich. They wanted me to park in the main section with the majority of campers. I explained to the woman at the check-in that I was looking for a really quiet spot as near to the water's edge as possible because I really needed some me time. She got one of the guys who works on the site to show me the perfect spot in the trees just a hundred yards from the edge of the loch. I was so grateful. It was perfect for me: not too busy.

I felt a bit anxious, which I always do when I arrive at a new place until I get my bearings. I plugged my van into the electrics and found where the water tap was. I filled my water canister and unpacked my fruit bowl, gins for the gin bar and various books and pictures that I put around the motorhome to make it feel more homely. It was very cold, so I wrapped up warm and headed off to explore my surroundings.

I could see the water through the trees. As I emerged I was so happy to see that there was a little beach area. This was perfect. It was even better than I had envisaged. I began tearing up. I knew what I needed was right here, and I was looking forward to spending a couple of weeks chilling and reflecting on the good and bad things in my life. I walked along the beach and on to the far side of the loch where I picked my way through the low-hanging branches of the trees to follow its edge. I just kept stopping to marvel at the views through the gaps in the trees. There were dark clouds looming in the distance so I decided to retrace my steps and head back to the sanctuary of my motorhome.

I knew that this part of my journey of self-discovery was all about trying to re-establish my self-worth, to reconnect with my true self. I wanted to realise my inherent value as a person. For too long now, as far back as my childhood, I had tried to prove myself to others, to gain their approval, even in some cases where I did not respect that person's perspective on life, but still needed their approval to make me feel worthy. I had even allowed my inner negative voice to compound the situation. When I spoke I sounded confident, but inside there was a completely different imposter-syndrome dialogue going on, so it was not hard for me to crumble when challenged. I would feel panicked, confused and angry. I knew that I was a good, kind person, willing to work hard. Why could life not see that and give me a break?

When I awoke the next morning and pulled open the blinds I was so happy to see the loch through the trees. I went for a walk. Thankfully there weren't many people around – the odd few walking their dogs on the beach. I kept myself very much to myself, deep in thought. I took my time and walked very slowly, not going too far because I wanted the time to absorb my beautiful surroundings. I found a nice-sized rock and plonked my bottom on that for a while, watching the ripples on the water. I wasn't really focusing much but I found it quite relaxing. I felt very emotional without really knowing why. I even shed a few tears when I thought about certain times in my life when I had felt lost and beaten. I felt better for starting to confront my emotions, as well as a little scared, because I didn't know exactly where all this was going to take me. It was something I knew I needed to do. I had come up here to the loch with the sole purpose of doing that. Was I going to be able to cope once I had opened the doors in my mind that I had kept firmly closed all these years?

I wandered back to the motorhome feeling exhausted.

A few nights later I headed out when it was very late and dark, but the moon, although not full, lit up the sky enough for me to find my way through the trees and along the narrow path along the side of the loch. I had to take a slight detour inland to get to the spot I had found a few days earlier. I still wasn't really sure what my intentions were in venturing out this late at night.

When I arrived at the edge of the loch I just stared up to the sky for what seemed like ages. I have always loved star-gazing. I thought I would start with a bit of self-reflection and meditation and see where that took me.

My mind was racing too much for me to really get into the meditation. I could feel sorrow and anger rising in my body that I was even having to do this. I started to think about my mother, who had died just months before I embarked on my motorhome madness. Tears began streaming down my cheeks and I cried quietly. I missed her with every bone in my body. I physically ached for her at times. I found myself saying out loud, 'Mum, help me, I'm lost, I wish you were here to talk to. How do I deal with these emotions and feelings swirling around inside me, that are stopping me from living the life I want and deserve?'

I began to sob, and as I sobbed my thoughts turned to my father. I had never really dealt with his death. The day after his funeral we went back to school and it was life as normal. I do remember vividly just sobbing my heart out in bed under the covers on one particular night, saying out loud, 'Oh Daddy, oh Daddy', and feeling totally bereft. But that was it. I just seemed to have shut a door because the feelings were too painful. I had so many things in my life that I wish he had been there for, and now here I was talking out loud to him, through my tears, wishing he was really here to answer. There was so much I wanted to ask him. I had a lot of anger about how he treated us as children, but as an adult I understood so much more about him. I wanted to feel love for him, not anger.

I also cried and grieved for my siblings, who I wished had lived longer. I missed them so much.

I went from feeling incredibly sad to gradually feeling very, very angry inside my head and heart as my thoughts turned to all the struggles I had had as a working single mother. I remember being judged by a boss once because I insisted on leaving work on time as I had to collect my daughter from school. It was as if that was a black mark against me. I remember having to work shifts that meant I had to leave Sammy to fend for herself when, in retrospect, she was really far too young. I was forced to compromise all the time. I was angry with myself now that I didn't speak up at the time and just say no. My belief in myself had been totally shaken. I had felt disempowered, afraid of losing my job and being unable to pay the mortgage and care for my daughter.

This brought to mind times when I felt I had been badly treated in the workplace, especially as I got older. I felt like I was going to burst with the strength of my emotions and I just spontaneously screamed out loud. It felt good. I didn't give a thought to whether someone could hear me in the distance, it just happened. Then I roared and cried and just let it all out. I completely let my emotions go. I was shaking, and I remember just sinking to my knees and having a really good cry, allowing myself to release the emotions. I had the conversations out loud with people who I felt had wronged me and told them what I thought; I asked how they would feel if a member of their family was treated that way, when all they wanted to do was an honest day's work to earn money to care for their child.

As quickly as I started crying it just stopped. I stayed there for ages, just feeling numb. I cannot remember if it was cold or not. I was just in the moment. Eventually I felt as if a massive weight had been lifted. There was a sense of peace and happiness. It sounds so crazy when only moments before I was howling like a mad woman and calling out all the things that had caused me pain in my life. I remember fumbling around to find tissues in my pocket and actually taking a deep breath and smiling as if to say to myself, 'You've done it, kiddo, it's going to be okay, you'll be alright.' I had no idea how or what I really meant with those thoughts. I then made my way slowly back to the motorhome feeling a bit shell-shocked, and a little bit embarrassed.

Even though I felt totally exhausted, it took me a while to drop off to sleep. I slept for hours, though. It wasn't until nearly midday the next day that I woke up. I had not done that for years. Usually I have to get up in the middle of the night for a pee at least. This time my body must have needed sleep.

I made myself a coffee, wandered down to the beach and found a rock to sit on. I watched the water rippling in the distance and reflected on what had happened the night before. I felt that it had been cathartic and I really did feel happier and lighter in myself already. I felt that I was no longer the same person mentally. I felt a sense of optimism about living my life positively and getting my message out there to inspire women both young and old.

I feel it is important for me to stress, too, that I acknowledge some men can also find this period of their lives difficult and often struggle to find their voice and their place in life, but I cannot speak for them. I can only relate my personal experiences. I am showing my journey, my ups and downs, in a bid to help women with their struggles. I want to show that these problems are not insurmountable.

I also determined that night that I would now use the painful memories as a positive, to put fire in my belly to live more positively. If these things hadn't happened to me then I wouldn't be feeling what I was in that moment. And it was a good feeling.

Rather than feel embarrassed about the screaming and shouting I had done last night I giggled to myself and thought I would tell everyone, 'If you're feeling pent up and have lots of emotions to deal with, I can highly recommend going to the side of a loch and letting it all out.'

I suddenly had a new and greater sense of my own self-worth. From now on I was going to be able to do things without worrying what others thought of me. As long as I was kind and loving it would be okay.

I will never forget my time at Loch Morlich because for me that is when the best phase of my life actually started.

Every morning I loved getting up and heading out to the edge of the loch, often with a cup of coffee in my hand. I would walk along to clear my head. The weather was so different every day, so I didn't tire of the views across the water because they were never the same. One day I watched as a snow storm made its way across the loch to where I was. I filmed it, presuming that it would take longer than it actually did and I got caught in it. It was also very windy, so the snow hitting my face at speed was not a pleasant experience. But I felt alive and at peace.

Feeling so much happier about life, I decided it was time for me to wrestle my bicycle off the bike rack once more and go for a ride to Aviemore along the Old Logging Way. It was only about five miles from the campsite into town.

With my new-found state of mind I felt like Snow White, cycling along listening to the birds and watching them flying around me as I pedalled through the trees. Snow-capped mountains in the distance just added to my total sense of freedom. I got a bit carried away and stood up on my pedals but soon stopped that when I nearly came a cropper! There wasn't much to see in Aviemore as most places were pretty quiet out of season. So I turned around and rode the five miles back again. En route I was fascinated by this beautiful big tree I cycled past. It looked like it had begun to fall over and its impressive roots were on display, showing how it was still connected to the earth and standing tall. The grit and determination to stay standing, even though its roots were exposed to the harsh elements, somehow struck a chord with me: the feeling of trying to establish roots; to be strong and dig down deep; to feel grounded in life.

It was time to move on. I was treated to the most breathtaking scenery as I drove for hours along the shore of Loch Ness, through Fort William and past Loch Leven, taking in the

Highlands of Ben Nevis and Glen Coe. The ski resort at Glen Coe was open but there wasn't enough snow for a good ski so I decided against it.

My heart felt so much lighter than when I had been driving up through Scotland a couple of weeks earlier. I just kept stopping and taking in my surroundings because they were so beautiful. The perk of my motorhome life is I can just pull over, park up, make myself a cup of tea, step outside and do a bit of sightseeing while sipping my brew. It makes me smile every time I do it. I can then carry on along the long and winding roads.

Around every corner the mountains, with their coverings of snow and dark, rusty shades, left me feeling so happy and at peace. I just kept thinking, 'This is what I've been dreaming of doing for years and it's actually happening!'

The beauty of exploring at this time of year is that there aren't too many people on the road, so I could take my time and drive slowly. I needed to get the most out of the Scottish landscape. I did not want to feel rushed. It would have been a lot harder for me to drive during the summer months when the roads are congested with tourists. I was still getting to grips with navigating the narrower roads in my large vehicle.

As if life couldn't get any better, when I approached Crianlarich on the edge of the Trossachs national park, I saw one of the most beautiful double rainbows I have ever seen in my life, to the left of me as I drove along towards Loch Lomond. I had to pull over immediately and rush out to take pictures.

It really felt like they were in touching distance, their colours were so vibrant. It seemed like a sign that life was going to be fabulous from here on in. It seemed to acknowledge that transition in my mindset from anger to optimism. I was literally overwhelmed and burst out crying with sheer happiness and joy. It was just such a perfect drive and a perfect day.

One of my closest friends, and my daughter's godmother, Nicola, just happened to phone me as I was crying. It was wonderful to chat to her and explain my emotions and what I was seeing. It is hard to put into words what that moment meant to me. I somehow felt it was a significant step in me finding myself and knowing that life has plenty more amazing things to show me in my retirement years.

I didn't want the moment to end and stood there for ages just staring at the best rainbows I had ever witnessed. Finally I jumped back into my motorhome and carried on my journey to the shores of Loch Lomond in southern Scotland.

I had this idea in my head of wild camping. I'd heard so much about people doing it, especially in Scotland. I felt it was maybe time to push my boundaries a bit. With this in mind I drove along looking for places to camp. In high season you are not allowed to wild camp without special permits and you have to stop at specific places along the shoreline. I hoped to find a nice spot. I admit I was very nervous about the whole idea. I would be facing one of my fears. Some of the places had already been taken when I got there. You snooze, you lose. These people seemed to know you had to get to your spot early.

I did pull into one place, then a dodgy-looking van appeared and I decided I wasn't brave enough yet to wild camp. I ended up driving to a designated campsite at the end of the loch. It wasn't my kind of thing really, as there were lots of caravans and motorhomes packed in on top of one another and I felt quite claustrophobic. I had got so used to being by lochs with hardly anyone around. But I thought I could put up with it for a couple of nights. I parked up and went for a wander down by the loch at sunset and was treated to a colourful sky which made the six-hour drive that day well worth it.

I know that I am lucky to be able to be totally selfish and do what I want to do, when I want to do it. It is liberating for me after so many years of being told what to do by people I didn't respect most of the time. A lot of women I have talked to experience similar things in the workplace and feel they have no other option than to retire before they would have liked. They feel powerless to speak up. They question the purpose of their lives. They lose their sense of identity. I want to do the opposite and really find out who I am and what makes me tick. I want to be my authentic self. Living this way in the motorhome is enabling me to follow that journey. It was a scary prospect heading out alone at the beginning, but already I was getting more of a sense of who I am. I have done a lot of soul-searching and taken a lot of inspiration from things I have read and like-minded people I have connected with on social media. In turn I hope it will inspire other women, especially those who may have lost their mojo during the menopause or lost their way when facing retirement and life's changes.

For me retirement is definitely an exciting phase of my life and I feel as if my life is moving forward and I am changing. I cannot wait to see what is in store for me along the way.

Chapter 11

Stopped in My Tracks

Just as I was beginning to make sense of things logistically with the motorhome and life on the road, as well as mentally after my life-changing experience by the loch, I started to read in the news about something called Covid. It apparently originated in China, and was now spreading across the world. There had been cases reported in Great Britain and they were rising at an alarming rate. It was a pandemic. People were afraid, including me. I didn't know what to do. I suddenly felt very alone and somehow vulnerable. I didn't know where to go as I no longer had a home. My daughter lived in a tiny flat in London with her boyfriend, so staying with her was not an option. What would I do with my motorhome? Besides, Dora the Explora was my home. I wanted to stay in her, wherever that would be. I had to find some place to base myself.

Heading down from Scotland I booked into a wonderful campsite in Moffat. I do some of my best thinking on walks, so I packed a snack and headed off into the beautiful Moffat Hills to decide my next course of action.

I have constantly said that I want to go with the flow and to have no plans. Sometimes life just gets in the way and you have to have a plan. This was one of those times. I decided to head to a site near my sister Liz, who lives near Lancaster. I had previously stayed there, so called the owner, Roger, and booked in.

When I heard about the first coronavirus fatality in the UK, I became increasingly anxious, especially as many people with whom I had come into contact were not taking the situation seriously. They seemed to think we would be okay and it was just some kind of flu that was only a danger to older people with underlying illnesses. My anxiety levels increased even more as I thought, 'Am I just being a drama queen? How can I see so clearly what's coming our way and yet so many other people can't?' I could not focus.

I got to the campsite in Lancaster just as there was talk of a lockdown to contain the spread of the virus. I felt very shaken up. At the same time I was dealing with the death of a niece at only thirty-two. The family were devastated. Sitting in my motorhome alone it was very hard to cope with my emotions. It made me feel so angry and powerless. I wanted to be there for my brother and his wife but wasn't able to go to them.

Roger was happy for me to stay on his site and spend lockdown there. I experienced the prejudice of some locals, though. They were not happy to see a motorhome in his field and presumed I was on holiday and not going back home. They called the police because they thought Roger hadn't closed his site, but when the police came to check, they agreed that I was alright to base myself there. I wasn't alone, though. There was a couple at the other side of the field who had just arrived from New Zealand: Helen and Steve.

They were born locally but had emigrated years ago to the other side of the world. This was supposed to be the trip of a lifetime for them. They were visiting her mother, who lived down the road, then supposedly heading off for a trip around Great Britain and Europe. They had picked up their brand new motorhome the day before and managed to do a mega shop in Ikea for all the things they might need. They luckily managed to place an order for ebikes too.

I stayed on the site throughout lockdown. After the initial fear I got into a happy routine of walks and bike rides to Morecambe Bay, many with Helen and Steve, who I told all about why I had decided to become a nomad. I even gave them advice and tips about van life. This made my brother Paddy laugh because I was constantly on the phone to him asking for advice. He would answer, 'Hello, Motorhome Helpline', then laugh his head off. I could not have survived the first few months without his invaluable support and patience when I felt overwhelmed with life on the road. So often women tell me they could not do what I have done. I say to them that it wasn't easy for me at first, but that's all part of the journey. You learn through the things you get wrong, and you realise that there are always people there to help you and guide you if you let them.

I had started this motorhome journey six months earlier without a real plan, but knowing somehow things would evolve and I would get my pro-age message out there. I would help change perceptions of what it is to be older; challenging organisations that play on women's insecurities about ageing; campaigning for more pro-age beauty products, better career opportunities for ageing women, etc. I had felt that I was slowly making some headway, gaining followers on social media, being told by women that I was inspiring them. I was talking on radio and podcasts about my motorhome madness, and writing for magazines. Now here I was, stopped in my tracks due to lockdown. It had certainly put paid to any plans to have people to stay in my motorhome so we could exchange stories about ageing. This was a big disappointment to me. After the initial shock of not being able to go anywhere, I was determined to still find ways to inspire women and speak out about ageism and ways to live better lives, especially in later life. I sent dozens of emails to anyone I thought would listen to my story of living life on the road with minimal belongings. Very few replied, but some did and that gave me the confidence to keep going.

As the country got to grips with the reality of Covid, I was glad to be isolated in Lancaster. My sister Liz was amazing. She did my shopping for me and left it at the barrier of the campsite so that we could social distance. I cried the first time she did it because all I wanted to do was go and give her a big hug, and I couldn't. We both admitted to feeling afraid of the unknown.

Eventually we did see the funny side of how she handed over my food, more importantly the bottles of wine! We would laugh so much about the absurdity of it all and how our lives were changing. The laughter was really the only way that we could deal with the situation.

Her house was only a couple of miles down the road from my motorhome. I would cycle past it on my daily bike ride. Even though I didn't see or speak to her, I felt reassured that she was so near. One day she took a sneaky photo of me pedalling past slowly on my bicycle and sent it to me.

Liz made fabulous food for me and left it in her porch for me to collect on my cycle rides. My favourite was her moussaka. My brother-in-law Keith would also leave me lots of fruit and veg from his allotment.

I was addicted to social media throughout lockdown. It stopped me feeling so scared and alone in my motorhome. The tribe of women I had built up would send me messages of support and we would discuss how life is for older women. I would hear about their struggles with work or the menopause. They were particularly cross about how older women are portrayed in newspapers and advertising, and they welcomed me trying to bring about change. I loved the feeling of women supporting women.

Rachel Peru, who encourages women to believe that they are enough and to be body confident as they age, has a podcast called *Out of the Bubble*. She interviewed me and it got a good response, which made me feel encouraged to keep on being a retirement rebel.

Family and friends also kept in regular touch, checking I was okay on my own during lockdown. Like half the nation, we set up a family Zoom quiz. I was the butt of the family jokes because I was useless at answering the questions and invariably came last. I did protest that I was alone and the others were in their family bubbles, so they could confer.

The daily bike rides were my saving grace, although it could get stressful when other cyclists got aggressive about which side I should be cycling on, and trying to navigate past walkers. One of my favourite activities was going to the virtual pub. Various groups that I was part of would call each other with a glass of something in hand and pretend we had met in the pub. It was a great way to stay connected.

I did miss hugging. I am known for hugging everyone. Some days I felt very low. Liz was great at making me feel better by sending me messages like the posters saying: 'Physical distancing NOT social distancing. We need each other more than ever right now.' I don't think she realised just what a support she was to me and other family members throughout lockdown. She often doubts what she does and loses herself at times, but I am in no doubt that what she did helped me get through that lockdown. I want her to know that she is one of the nicest, kindest people, and for her family she is an unsung hero.

As the weeks passed there were moments when I felt my efforts to be heard were pointless. Who did I think I was? Who would want to listen to what I had to say? Then a magazine would call or someone would ask me to write something for their blog and I would be reinvigorated and fire off another load of emails to anyone I could think of, like *Woman's Hour*, *Loose Women* and national papers and magazines.

For years I had gone on about how we are losing perspective in life. We all work hard to buy stuff that we don't really need. We focus too much on work to pay for material things, meanwhile having very little time left for loved ones. We are losing that human contact and fun, all for money and STUFF! I hoped that when we surfaced from lockdown people would realise the importance of family and friends and not focus on material things so much.

I was even connecting with nature more by listening to the birds on my early bike rides. The lack of cars just accentuated the birdsong. It made me miss my mother even more because she always tried to teach me about the birds and I didn't take it in. How I wished she was by my side, telling me what birds were singing their beautiful songs.

I came a cropper on one of my bike trips, trying to keep socially distanced and avoid a man in the road. I decided to move to the other side and hop on to the pavement with my bike, like an accomplished cyclist. There were two flaws in my plan: firstly the pavement was far too high; secondly I was not an accomplished bike rider! So the upshot was I hit the pavement at speed, went flying over the handlebars and crashed to the ground, hitting my head on a wall. Thank goodness I was wearing a cycle helmet!

The fella stood still initially, then came running over to see if I was okay, but I had to call out, 'No! No! Move away, don't come over! We need to stay apart.' I sat there battered, bleeding and bruised in a heap on the pavement. I was in shock. I knew I needed to make my way back to the motorhome on my own as I couldn't call anyone. I managed to scramble to my feet and try to stem the flow of blood from my hand and not think about the pain. The handlebars were bent at forty-five degrees to the front wheel, but I managed to tentatively cycle it back home with the battery on full to help me.

I shocked the landowner and his wife when they saw me pedalling up the driveway covered in blood and with a bent bike. Fortunately for me, Roger was able to straighten it as I took myself off to tend to my wounds. I had battered my knee and had several cuts and bruises on my arms and legs, and a corker of a black eye. I pretty much stayed in my motorhome for several days in complete shock. I realised that I was also suffering from concussion. I used plenty of ice packs and painkillers, but everything was still very sore and the bruising came out all over my body. If I am honest, I felt a bit of an idiot. What was I thinking by ever attempting that manoeuvre in the first place?

Thankfully my fab neighbours on the site, Helen and Steve, looked out for me and got my shopping and checked my concussion didn't get any worse. My sister bought booze and chocolate to cheer me up.

Stuck in the motorhome, I decided to do gentle exercise with some weights, which in retrospect was silly because there isn't much room. I bashed my already-damaged left hand with one of the weights. It was extremely painful and swelled up. It seemed my body was telling me to just stop for a while. The most I did for a good few days was gentle walks.

One thing I had noticed during lockdown was that some of the coronavirus debates in the media seemed to pit the younger and older generations against one another. I liked that I could share my feelings with like-minded people on social media and gauge their opinions on how older people were being treated in lockdown. Many didn't like what they saw. It just put more fire in my belly to keep on fighting ageism and stereotypes of retired women in society for the foreseeable future.

I also loved to feel that my comments and meanderings may have been of some comfort and support to others during that crazy time.

After a couple of months, I realised I was beginning to struggle mentally, mainly due to the fear of the unknown. I was trying to adapt to a new normal, living with restrictions, when what I had embarked on was free-spirited. I had made changes to my lifestyle, wearing masks, sanitising my hands and keeping a social distance. My sleep was totally disrupted and I felt tired and sluggish. I was frustrated at not being able to continue on my journey, especially as I had now managed to get articles in both *Platinum* and *Simply You* magazines.

After a while I struggled to even remember what day of the week it was, safe in my bubble hiding away from the threat of the coronavirus. One of the things I hated most was the feeling of loss of control over my life at a time when I wanted to take back control of every aspect of it.

Before all the restrictions started I used to regularly get my grey roots coloured at the hairdresser's, but since lockdown I had watched them grow. For a nanosecond I considered going grey, but I just could not do it. There are those who feel that if you age positively, you should embrace the grey. I say to them, the way I age positively is by feeling good when I colour my hair. I do not feel good allowing the grey to come through. It is a personal choice.

Thankfully when I was packing the motorhome I put two boxes of hair colour in a locker in case of emergencies. Well, this was most definitely my emergency. I took myself off to the shower block on the site and set to colouring it. I was amazed at just how easy it was to do and with the final results. I felt myself becoming a convert to DIY hair dyeing in the future, and it would save me a bob or two. I know it sounds silly, but just dyeing my hair gave me a new lease of life and I felt more energised and positive about things.

As lockdown came to an end, I tried to envisage life as we moved more freely. Part of me wanted the freedom to carry on exploring Great Britain and meet new people. The other part of me wanted to be in my safe place in the field away from everyone.

I had had plenty of time over the last few months to think long and hard about how I would take my campaigning forward. I had been concerned at calls for over-sixties to stay inside to help contain Covid. I was incensed. I understand that it is vital that people who need support get it, but those who don't should not be made to adhere to government commands because they have reached a certain age. No doubt in the future I will be grateful for extra support in situations like this as my health and body become less robust. But for now I am able to climb mountains, cycle and walk for miles, and I would say I am fit for a woman in her sixties. Okay, I have a bit of a dodgy knee that gives me gip, but that doesn't mean I should be herded into the vulnerable category. So moving forward, I want people to look at the issue of ageism at all ages, because it doesn't just affect the elderly. Ageism means that you are discriminated against because of your age. So younger people can come up against it too. It is something we should all be aware of and address it when we see it happening.

Older people are widely patronised and mocked in society and many are seen as incompetent. This needs to be addressed, particularly in the workplace. The government is forcing us to work longer and wait longer to get our pensions, but at the same time attitudes in the workplace are not changing quickly enough. The last few years in my job I felt that I had to fight hard to get my voice heard. Older workers can be wrongly perceived by poor managers as having lower levels of performance and feel forced out of their jobs. They become so stressed they cannot fight the ageism any more. I can relate to that. There needs to be more awareness in society, and even more legislation, to prevent this from happening. As pension ages rise, women who feel they have to leave work early because of ageism are literally being forced into poverty, and that must not happen.

Advertising, marketing and the media should rethink their narratives and use positive visual representations of people over fifty, sixty and beyond. We want to see them embrace ageing and celebrating being older. Instead of vibrant women who love life, often we are reduced to body parts – wrinkled hands, white hair. This has to change. Women need to have role models to aspire to. They need to see that there are alternative ways to get old and that a mindset change can improve your prospects of enjoying life. Being 'old' is a positive, not a negative.

I felt more confident that I would be able to help change perceptions. I was currently doing it, so I felt many other people could too. I was eager to continue my motorhome travels as a retired pensioner the moment I could move freely. I wanted to shout from the treetops that life is for living. From the day we are born we are ageing, whether we like it or not – some faster than others and some for longer than others. Ageing is a privilege that we should embrace and make the most of, without restriction. We must put ourselves where we want to be, not where society says we should be because we have reached a certain number of years on this planet.

* * *

One thing I learnt in lockdown was that during my future travels I would need to stop in places a little longer and give myself time to actually get to know an area. Often I would stay one or two nights in a spot, then move on. If it were not for lockdown, I would probably have spent only a few days in Lancaster and I would have missed so much of its beauty. There are so many exciting cycle routes to explore, especially to the coastline around Morecambe Bay and along the canal, where I would have to dodge the feisty swans as I navigated my way past the beautifully decorated canal boats.

Being in my lockdown bubble may have lulled me into a false sense of security. My anxiety returned with a vengeance as the time came for the campsite to open and the public to return. I was worried and excited in equal measure because I did want things to return to normal, whatever normal was now. I hoped the people who arrived on the site would respect the distance rules and keep things clean and tidy so as not to put others at risk. My lockdown buddies and I had taken it in turns each week to give the toilet block a thorough cleaning with bleach and disinfectant, so I hoped that standards would be maintained.

As soon as the site opened, some of my family came in their motorhomes and tents, and we had a great few days together reconnecting. I hadn't seen Sammy for over six months and I physically ached to see her. She drove up from London with her boyfriend and Frank the dog to pitch their tent alongside my motorhome. It was so emotional for us all to be together again after so long. I realised just how much I needed my family and friends in my life. I have learnt that I'm not as strong mentally without them. I thought I would be able to deal with lockdown okay. I coped physically, heading out on my ebike to explore, but mentally I had some pretty dark days where I cried for no reason – really heart-wrenching cries because I missed the human and physical contact that feeds my soul. Saying that, I know I am fundamentally a strong woman. I am proud of the things I have overcome in my life and I know that I can overcome so much with the support of family and friends.

I had decorated all around my motorhome with balloons, bunting and lanterns and the others decorated their setups so that it was like a mini Glastonbury Festival. We laughed, we cried and we had lots to eat and drink. It filled our souls with love and warmth again. We all needed that bit of family bonding after lockdown.

I was ready to hit the road again. My plan as always was to have no plan. I would just let my mood take me to places. I would look at the maps, pick out places I fancied exploring: if I liked it I would stay a while and if not I would move on. That feeling of doing what I want, when I want, was what I missed in lockdown. Freedom of thought and movement were the main motivating factors for me taking to the road in the first place.

I was thrilled to hear that some women had actually gone and bought themselves campervans after seeing what I was doing. It made me feel happy that they were inspired to have their own adventures. Some listened to me chatting to Pat Marsh on BBC Radio Kent about my motorhome madness. He is following my progress on this life journey.

Roger and his wife Sarah kindly did a wonderful farewell barbecue for the 'Lockdown Crew', as we had been nicknamed. It was a great way to say our goodbyes and to reflect on what life had been like for us all during the five months of lockdown and how we all supported one another through good and bad times.

I admit that as I prepared to drive off the site I felt anxious about what life was going to be like. I had bottles of hand sanitiser and wet wipes in all my bags and in the front of the motorhome so I could grab them at a moment's notice, as well as masks and gloves. I felt prepared.

It was time for me to move on. My dream destination would have been the Outer Hebrides. I had read so much about them all my life. I saw them as my happy place, but for various reasons I had still not made it that far north. It would have been the perfect antidote to lockdown. But to begin with, post-lockdown, I headed to familiar places. I stayed on my brother's driveway in Lincolnshire and then travelled over the Humber Bridge to catch up with friends I had made when I worked at BBC Radio Humberside. I had booked a site, but one of my friends, Gillie, insisted I park my motorhome in her front garden. When I rocked up she did admit that she didn't realise just how big it was going to be, but all the same I got a warm welcome. 'Come and relax with me,' she said ... not mentioning that meant dragging me to her personal training session, gym workout, yoga and on bike rides and long dog walks. I became a lot fitter and ready to continue my positive-ageing van life.

I continued my travels and prayed I wouldn't get stopped in my tracks again by another lockdown. I would meet up with friends along the way but mainly in outside areas at pubs and restaurants. Instead of hugging, which I instinctively wanted to do, we would bump fists or elbows, and I started to get on with some semblance of normal life. I was still not really sure what that entailed yet. As happy as I was to catch up with people, I just could not shake my underlying feeling of sadness and anxiety. I wondered if anyone else felt the same. I was somewhat reassured when the response on social media was an overwhelming agreement that people felt slightly sad and anxious about the future. I tried to suppress my anxiety and remain optimistic that somehow things would work out for the best. If it didn't, then I would deal with the fallout and move on. It is still unknown territory for us all.

I felt I needed grounding, so I headed for a site near Sammy's home. A sleepover with her and Frank the dog would be perfect medicine. Frank always adored time with his 'grand-pawrent' too. We both get ridiculously excited when we see one another. It was just what I needed: quality time with Sammy, chatting with each other about how lockdown had impacted us – the good and the bad bits. We talked about how rubbish I was in the family quiz nights; how her life had changed because she had bought her first flat in Tunbridge Wells during lockdown and was now working from home – all very stressful things combined together. I am so proud of how she copes with life. Yes she gets anxious, but she finds a way through it and and has a fab group of friends to talk through her worries with. If I am honest, I think she does also worry about me being on the road in my van. I try my best to allay her fears. Hopefully the longer I do it, the better she will feel.

Chapter 12

Go Home?! This Is My Home!

I was beginning to experience the underlying feeling of anxiety I had had before the announcement of the first lockdown. Every day the incidence of people with Covid was rising, and reports in the news seemed to indicate that we were heading for another lockdown. Many campsite owners decided it was far too risky to open. I was beginning to struggle to find places to stay and feel safe at the same time. By mid-October 2020, the government introduced a tier system to try and contain the rise in cases. Not long afterwards I was exploring Norfolk, a tier-two area, which meant minimal restrictions. I had arranged to meet up with my brother Paddy and his wife, Lorraine, in their motorhome, and with my other sister-in-law, who is also called Lorraine, in her campervan, in Wells-next-the-Sea. As always, Paddy was fantastic at giving me advice when I called him up asking what I should do to stay safe in my motorhome. He really was still my 'Motorhome Helpline' on the other end of the phone. I know that I recharge my batteries when I am around my family, and now more than ever I needed that connection with them.

We had great fun exploring the port town of Wells-next-the-Sea, although we were wary about going into crowded places and kept our distance as we wandered around. I could feel there was a certain level of unease among us, all of us unsure about safety. None of us voiced our concerns, but it was definitely hanging in the air. We walked from the town to the long, sandy beach where we were greeted by a row of colourful beach huts on stilts. It was beautiful.

We had a lovely few days just relaxing with one another before they headed home. I moved further along the coast to Blakeney, a beautiful coastal village within the Area of Outstanding Natural Beauty and the North Norfolk Heritage Coast, with Lorraine. We checked into a certified location site not too far from the harbour and spent a few days going for walks and exploring Cley next the Sea, where there is a wonderful windmill which has been converted into a boutique hotel.

We even got the coastal bus to Cromer, although I was pretty uptight because I was trying to keep away from people as much as I could. I loved the long walk along its sandy beach, which, much to my delight, was nearly deserted. Even the Grade-II-listed pier, which houses the Pavilion Theatre – closed due to the pandemic – had very few people on it as they were reluctant to venture outdoors, so I let Lorraine persuade me to stroll along the length of it. For a while I forgot my fears, looking out over the sea and watching the seagulls dive-bombing into the sea to catch their fish. Later that day my fears abruptly resurfaced again as the government confirmed that it was introducing a second lockdown at the start of November. I never envisaged that a pandemic would stop me in my tracks once, let alone twice. We chatted about what was the best course of action. Lorraine headed home to Harrogate and I began to panic. Once again, what should I do? Where should I go?

I called James and Serena, who owned the site that I was currently staying on just outside Blakeney. There were no other vans there. I explained my situation and asked if they would be okay with me staying there during lockdown. Luckily they happily agreed, even though they were shutting the site down. Apparently I fitted the Caravan and Motorhome Club criteria for being allowed to remain because my motorhome was my home, I was working as a freelance journalist from it, I had been there before lockdown started and I had nowhere else to go. I felt like I could breathe again and that I would be okay. In my head I planned that for the next few months I would keep my head down and stay safe. I would try to put all that was happening into perspective and not lose myself or be overwhelmed, like I did at times in the first lockdown. It would just be another twist to my story. I was determined to conquer all the difficulties I would face, even the constant battle with my anxiety about what was going to happen next. This was not my idea of going with the flow, having no plan at all and being free. It was quite the opposite.

Settling into lockdown in the field was not without its troubles. Some of the locals were not happy I was there, even though I wasn't doing them any harm. They knew that campsites had been shut down all around the country. When they saw my motorhome parked up in the field they obviously questioned why I was still there, presuming I was still on holiday. One chap who was walking his dog nearby persisted in calling out, 'Oy, you shouldn't be here. Go home. We don't want you here, go away.'

I retorted with, 'This is my home! Just make sure you have all the facts before you start shouting at me.' He continued calling out and intimidating me.

I was left feeling extremely unnerved and very frightened. My mind started working overtime. I pictured him coming into the field to harass me and maybe even attack my motorhome. I feared for my safety and wondered if what I was doing was foolhardy. In all the months that I had been travelling, which was well over a year by now, I had not felt this frightened by anything. When I saw James the next day, planting new trees along the edge of the field, I told him what had happened. He was not happy. Fortunately for me, James was very supportive. He was angry that I was being treated this way and said, 'You don't have to explain yourself to anyone. Tell them to call us and we'll put them straight.' Serena gave me their personal phone number to contact them day or night if I needed to. It was so nice to have this level of support from people I had only just met. I do believe that kindness is such a strength of character, and I was so fortunate to have come across this kind couple at a time when I was feeling vulnerable.

James also put locks on the main gate to the field and a sign saying the area was closed due to government restrictions. He told me that he had done all the checks to make sure I could stay during lockdown. They even helped me with my food shopping. Serena did a weekly Asda shop, and she told me to send her a list of things I needed and she would just add it to her order. I would send her pictures of food items I needed, along with wine and gin to restock my gin bar. She would then let me know how much I owed her and I would transfer the payment to her via online banking. Later that day she would text me to say that the shopping had arrived. She would then put it into bags and leave them outside her door for me to collect. Sometimes she would be there in the doorway and it was nice to have a good chat with her at a distance. She did say that locals had been asking who I was and what I was doing there, and she had let them know that I was there legitimately. She said people were getting used to the idea and the bad feelings were subsiding. James and Serena had gone out of their way to make sure I was alright and I will never forget their kindness. It is exactly how I would have treated someone in my position. I will never get used to mean-spirited people.

I couldn't move my motorhome out of the field or drive anywhere because of the lockdown restrictions. This is when my ebike was a godsend. I was able to get out on it most days and explore the North Norfolk coastline. I questioned why I hadn't been here before as it was so breathtakingly beautiful. The nature reserve is a haven for all kinds of birds, most of which, I have to be honest, I don't know the names of; but that didn't stop me enjoying their beauty as flocks flew above my head, dancing around in the sky. The North Norfolk coastal path ran alongside the field I was parked up in. Walkers would stop and stare at me in the field. No doubt they too wondered why I was there.

I did befriend one couple from the village who regularly came to the field to see that I was okay and to chat. They had been camping alongside me for a few nights prior to lockdown because they were having some work done on their house nearby. They had decided to decamp to their motorhome to avoid the mess and inconvenience of no water and electricity. I got chatting to them and it turned out that they had travelled a lot when they were younger. He was called Colin Miller and is a very famous and renowned sculptor. He had his studio not far from the site. I googled him and loved some of his abstract pieces. Both he and his wife, Diana, took a genuine interest in what I was doing and in the articles I was writing for magazines and newspapers to champion positive ageing and to show that you can be happy with very little. They would stand all wrapped up and I would stand in the doorway of my motorhome, keeping a social distance as we chatted. They had a fascinating story themselves. They had lived and worked in Greece for many years in the 1960s before coming back to live in the UK. Over the next four and a half months they regularly came across to chat and see how things were going. They told me about their daughter who was a doctor and their son who worked in the film industry. We all worried about how Covid restrictions were keeping us from seeing our loved ones.

We compared how isolation was going for us. They expressed their sympathy that I had been subjected to a barrage of unpleasant comments at the beginning of lockdown and explained that the bad feelings stemmed from some people who had second homes in the area. They had been sneaking up from London, and locals felt this was putting them at risk, so understandably they may have felt threatened by anyone they didn't think belonged there. I stuck out like a sore thumb in my motorhome, so therefore I was a target. That had all died down now and months later, I was almost a local.

I was so grateful for their visits. They really cheered me up and I was grateful for the interaction, even though I had talked regularly on Zoom with friends and family. There is nothing like the real interaction of talking face to face for lifting your spirits.

This lockdown was different from the last one because it was winter. The sun would set at ten to four and the long, dark winter nights in the van did take their toll at times, so talking was important for me. I pretty much kept myself to myself. I was lucky that over the next few weeks I was able to walk for miles, sometimes as far as Blakeney Point to watch the seals coming up on to the beaches. The winter sunshine shone most days and I loved looking at the cloud formations in the blue winter skies as I walked along the sea defences to Cley. The view of the eighteenth-century windmill in the distance and nearby nature reserve filled my heart with joy. Despite its name, Cley has not been next to the sea since the seventeenth century, due to land reclamation. But the walk from the windmill to the shingle beach is wonderful, and I loved to sit on the beach and reflect on what I had done, what I was doing and what I hoped to achieve.

There is also the Grade-I-listed medieval church of St Margaret. Its nave dates from 1320–40, and it is amazing to see all the bits that have been added on to it through the years. I took a good walk around it to really appreciate its beauty and its imposing structure. I noticed that a lot of the buildings in Cley have Flemish-style gables, and that stems from when it was once one of the busiest ports in England and did a lot of trade with the Low Countries. There is a wonderful pottery where normally you can see them making pots through the window; nearby is a small smokery. It was sad to see them shut as I wandered by.

During my walks through the nature reserve I used my binoculars to spot the wide variety of birds arriving and taking off from the area. My mother would have been proud, as she loved birdwatching and I had never really got it until now. Maybe that was because for the first time in my life I actually had the time to stand and stare, to take in my surroundings and all that nature has to offer. One of the benefits of lockdown was that I was getting to see this beautiful part of the country without hordes of tourists blocking the streets and pathways.

The downside, though, was not being able to find out more about the history of the place and chat to locals. I had heard that people who have grown up here for generations are very protective of their surroundings and that some feel pushed out because so many outsiders are buying up the beautiful properties as second homes, forcing them to move away because they cannot afford to buy near their families.

During the second lockdown I had continued to write articles about ageism and positive ageing for magazines and newspapers. Despite this, I was finding it much harder being a retirement rebel in lockdown, second time around. The winter months and much shorter days took their toll mentally and physically. I was determined to also read up more about ageism and learn from and engage with people on social media. It was refreshing to see and hear so many older women who were not just letting life happen *to* them. They, like me, were making life happen *for* them, and loving it.

There is no question that ageing does have its hindrances for some – slowing down, aching joints, etc. – but it certainly has many benefits. As I get older and bolder I want to help to change the narratives surrounding ageing and show a more positive side to it. Ageing is a blessing and a privilege. What is the alternative? I have seen many family members die far too young and I cherish the time I have to live life to the full. I try to make every day count. During the second lockdown, seeing so many suffering because of the impact of coronavirus heightened even more for me the importance of living life and embracing every day we wake up. I realised that I don't need lots of stuff to make me happy as I age; I need to make memories and have experiences. This became increasingly hard and I had some good cries because of the fear and frustration I felt at times. I couldn't fathom out how I was going to get my life back on track. I managed after the first lockdown, but this time it felt like an uphill battle.

Then my spirit came back fighting; I could see a way forward and realised that I had to rethink my goals. I continued to read as much as I could about the impact of the ageing process on all of us. I contributed to discussions on social media; I engaged with webinars involving people from marketing and the media. One of my bugbears is 'anti-ageing' creams: we are all ageing so lotions and potions should enhance that process; make us look good whatever our age. We have to expose ageist attitudes, no matter how trivial it seems, so that people in advertising and the media, along with big corporate companies, stop getting it so wrong.

Saying that, I can feel the winds of change and I am encouraged that the message is trickling through that we age differently nowadays. More older women are engaging on social media about what needs to be done to get their voices heard and to make sure that life doesn't pass them by. I just love that adventurous spirit.

Even after this, though, I have to admit to struggling. The Covid-19 restrictions and the long, dark winter nights played heavily on my mind. Increasingly it became harder to motivate myself to write my blog and engage on social media as much as I had been doing. Things I had planned to do, like inviting people to join me on the road for a couple of nights to experience the freedom and beauty, had fallen by the wayside because of the restrictions imposed.

This left me feeling lost for a while, without a sense of purpose. I was also finding my way on social media and realised that I had to develop a thick skin if I was to interact with some elements of it. There are some very strong opinions out there. On the whole I would observe debates rather than be drawn into them. I needed to stay focused on my goal.

I have to say I was thrilled when I passed the 1,000 followers mark on my Twitter account, @siobhandaniels, and that I was gaining a strong following on Instagram at @shuvonshuvoff. This gave me renewed vigour for my travels. It is nice to know I am inspiring people to want to hit the road in retirement and on the whole I love the interaction I have with people on social media. There is an amazing tribe of women who support each other in their endeavours. I have been a guest blogger for some, written magazine articles for others, given talks to groups, joined webinar discussions and book clubs along the way. All this combined helped me combat the difficult periods.

* * *

I felt at home in Blakeney. There were always people dotted about staring through their binoculars, trying to catch a glimpse of the various migrating birds. I could see lots of signs for seal boat trips and places to fish for crabs. But there was no one around to join in those activities. It was so quiet in the harbour area.

Having lived in places all my life that are full of light pollution, one thing that never failed to excite me was opening the door of the motorhome and gazing up at the stars in the pitch black.

I would wrap up warm, grab a blanket, a hot water bottle and a cup of tea, and sit on the step of the van and just stargaze. I have even been treated to shooting stars and made a few wishes. One of my wishes was for Sammy and Frank the dog to join me for a few days over Christmas, and it looked like it could happen. I was beyond excited and had even gone out and bought a tub of Quality Street. (I did also get a Terry's Chocolate Orange but succumbed to temptation and ate it all in one sitting.)

I had begun planning what we would eat for our Christmas dinner and what silly games we would play, like Hide the Thimble. I wanted to make it as much fun as possible, even though I knew that, like many others, we were anxious about the Covid situation.

Well, a couple of days after publishing my blog about Sammy coming to spend Christmas with me, the Prime Minister announced far tighter restrictions, which meant she couldn't come. I had dreamt of my daughter and I laughing and having the luxury of time together in the motorhome. I had decorated it especially for her. I was craving a hug from her and being with family. When this was taken away so suddenly I sobbed for ages and felt quite bereft. I had so wanted to see her. Even though it would only have been for a few days I know it would have seemed like a lifetime for both of us. It just seemed so unfair.

Then I stopped myself in my tracks and realised that I am better off than a lot of people and it was just one thing we had to do to ensure that we had a long-term future. It didn't make it any easier, but I had to resign myself to Christmas alone. This was just another bump in life's road that I had to find a way to navigate. I told her not to worry and that it was better to be safe than sorry.

I managed to bundle up her pressie and post it at the local village post office, which was still opening. They were very friendly with me and asked how I was doing in my motorhome and wished me well. It is wonderful how a bit of kindness can make one feel so much better. As I walked back to the field I found myself smiling and happy that the locals seemed to care that I was okay. What a contrast from twenty-four hours ago when I was sobbing uncontrollably because I would not be seeing Sammy that Christmas.

To be honest, I made the best of things on Christmas Day and ended up having a lovely day. The owners of the field, James and Serena, invited me to their house for a Christmas drink. I wrapped up warm and they left a drink outside for me at a safe distance and we chatted through the open doors. Back at the motorhome I opened my presents that family and friends had posted to the farm for me, as I FaceTimed and Zoom-called them. Sammy had sent me a bottle of champagne which I drank slowly throughout the day. I felt quite spoilt.

As the new year approached, I was taking a long walk to reflect on the year that had passed, trying to work out my aims for the coming year, when I spotted a tiny bunch of snowdrops. I just stopped in my tracks and smiled. 'They're optimistic,' I thought, 'with this cold weather.' I determined then that I would take a leaf out of their book: for the next 365 days, whatever came my way, I would make the most of it, plough through and flourish.

The government announced a vaccination programme and I needed to figure out how to get mine because I didn't want to miss out. I registered as a temporary patient with a local doctor's surgery. They said it would be several weeks before I would be called in to get it. I also kept checking on the government website, but the nearest vaccination centre was about fifteen miles away. I knew I would be able to cycle there but wasn't sure how I would be after the vaccine for cycling back. When I mentioned this to Serena one day as I picked up my shopping, without hesitation she said, 'Just book it, I'll take you. Jim and I have had ours and you can sit in the back of the car with a mask on, and you're in our bubble anyway.' So I booked it and two days later she drove me to get the vaccine, waited outside and drove me straight back to my field. Thankfully I didn't have any reaction to it, and felt relieved that I had had it.

Life's journey can be difficult at the best of times. I had expected to be travelling around Great Britain freely in my motorhome. The reality was, I was stuck in a field in tier four.

For a while I lost my mojo and sense of direction. I questioned myself and what I was doing. I had pretty much made up my mind at one stage that I would sell up and go back to living a settled life in a flat and write and campaign about ageing issues. Then out of the blue I was contacted by several people for various reasons, but one thing they all had in common was that they were inspired by what I was doing and followed my story with interest. I realised I had to stop feeling sorry for myself, dust myself down, re-evaluate my situation. I knew that when I had retired and decided to live 'the van life' while travelling around Great Britain, I always wanted to meet adventurous, creative and ambitious older women in their fifties, sixties, seventies and beyond and to tell their stories. That was impossible with Covid restrictions. I had to have a good rethink about what I could feasibly do. I did not want to be beaten by the pandemic.

As I was stuck in one place in my motorhome – a beautiful place, I might add – on the North Norfolk coast, where I was lucky that I could get out for walks and cycle rides to some beautiful places, I had to embrace technology and bring the people to me. I decided that I would do weekly Instagram lives with some of the inspirational women I had begun to follow and befriend on social media. I wanted to have relaxed conversations about the highs and lows of what spurs them on to embrace ageing and to do the things they do.

I was thrilled when Jo Moseley, @healthyhappy50, who is in her late fifties, agreed to be my first guest. She is a mother of two boys in their twenties and lives on the edge of the beautiful Yorkshire Dales. She describes herself as a 'beach cleaner, joy encourager and midlife adventurer'. As soon as I saw that, I was hooked. I wanted to know more about this woman and her adventures. We had the most wonderful evening talking about her film, *Brave Enough – A Journey Home to Joy*, and her podcast, *The Joy of SUP – The Paddleboarding Sunshine Podcast*.

In August 2019, Jo became the first woman to stand-up paddleboard (SUP) the 162 miles from coast to coast across northern England, along the Leeds and Liverpool Canal, and the Aire and Calder Navigation. She was picking up litter along the way to fundraise for *waveproject.co.uk*, which helps young people improve their emotional and physical well-being, and for The 2 Minute Foundation, which encourages people to take just two minutes of their time to pick up some litter at a beach or any waterway. *Brave Enough – A Journey Home to Joy* is the result.

From the moment I saw Jo's face pop up on the screen for the Instagram live, I felt a connection, and it was such a joy to get to know more about her story. She candidly told me about how she had been single-handedly looking after her two boys, who were teenagers at the time, as well as supporting her elderly parents. Unbeknown to her, she was also perimenopausal, and she became overwhelmed by her life and eventually broke down crying in a supermarket. Thankfully one of her friends suggested she take up some form of exercise to help her sleep better. She started on a rowing machine and says that after a few weeks she 'found herself' again. Eventually she had her first paddleboarding lesson in 2016 and hasn't looked back since. She says that putting on her wetsuit is like 'putting on my cape. I feel good, I feel safe.'

She initially came up with the idea of the coast-to-coast SUP adventure in 2016 but put it on the back burner, due to her lack of confidence. Then, two years later, thanks to a meeting with a man in a caravan park, which she described very amusingly, she planned her 2019 SUP trip, including picking up litter along the way to highlight the use of single-use plastics. Jo teamed up with filmmaker Frit Tam, @frit_tam, who she had met at an adventure festival. She described how Frit was there most days to capture all the emotions of the trip, even when she burst into tears because she had gone wrong and ended up doing more miles because she had to retrace part of her route. But, thankfully, she never fell into the canal.

I then went on to interview another dozen women from as far afield as the US, Ireland and France over the course of a few months. Hundreds of people watched them, reassuring me that my message about alternative ways to age was getting out there and being heard. I wanted more women to not be afraid but to dig deep and find their inner courage to say yes more to adventure, whatever form that adventure took.

Since I set off on my motorhome journey around Great Britain eighteen months earlier, there had been the worst storms, with storms Brendan and Dennis being particularly harsh, the most rainfall in February 2020 since records began, and a pandemic. As if that was not enough for me to contend with, February 2021 provided me with 'extreme' weather conditions. Some of the lowest temperatures in the country since the 1960s were recorded, as low as -23° Celsius at one of the weather stations.

I did not let this keep me in the motorhome, though. I wrapped up warm and went for long walks along the sea defences to Morston. I revelled in the sheer delight of cracking the ice on the frozen puddles. People laughed at me as they passed by, watching this mad woman crunching ice beneath her feet. But I did chuckle to myself and wonder just how many of them would have a go themselves on the next puddle they came across. It was so liberating taking time to do the little things I did as a child before life got in the way.

When I started seeing pictures of snow in other parts of the country I really wanted it to head for North Norfolk. I wanted to see the beauty of the white stuff all around my motorhome. I had a romanticised view of what it would be like. Saying that, I also made contingency plans in case the temperatures plummeted too much and the water supply pipe froze. I filled my tank to the top and my spare water container and two of my cooking pans. I felt well prepared.

The first morning when I opened the blind of the motorhome and peered outside and saw that it had been snowing, I could not contain my excitement. I ran outside in my pyjamas and took lots of photographs and messaged my daughter. I felt like a child on Christmas Day – even though the snow was not very deep.

All that changed over the following few days. There were heavy snow storms and winds of up to fifty miles an hour to contend with, which made it pretty tough being inside the motorhome at night. I honestly felt that the thing might blow over, despite lots of people telling me I was bottom heavy! Thankfully that was not an insult referring to my frame. It was because my tank was full of water, the engine was heavy and my motorhome was packed with lots of my belongings.

Several feet of snow finally settled and it really did look very picturesque. I loved making virgin footprint tracks in the snow around the field. I spent one afternoon making a snowwoman. It was the best feeling in the world. I felt so happy and it reminded me of the times I made snowmen with Sammy when she was little. My snowwoman looked so cute, I would find myself talking to her through the window. Over several days I would check that she was still there. I was quite sad when she eventually melted.

The only downside of the freezing conditions was that my water supply pipe outside froze almost straight away. I was glad that I had a full water tank. I was able to have hot showers, but after a few days that water supply ran out – just as the pipes in the motorhome froze. If I am honest, I panicked at first, thinking they would burst when they defrosted. It is times like this that I feel a bit stressed being on my own. Women who contact me say they too would be afraid on their own, especially when things go wrong. This is why I want to show them that I am just the same as them. I have no option but to face my fears and sort the problem. I found some thermal underwear and wrapped it around the pipes, put the water heating on and turned the heating up in the motorhome, and kept my fingers crossed.

Meanwhile I was gathering snow in pans and melting it for making tea and coffee and for boiling up to have strip washes. I was pretty proud of myself and felt I could relate more to Bear Grylls now. This made me chuckle to myself. My brother gave me one tip: 'Do not collect the yellow snow', which he thought was hilarious advice.

Eventually the novelty of the snow began to wear off. It was grubby and half melted and very icy in places. I hadn't minded the cold at first, wrapping up warm in blankets and using my hot water bottle. Now I didn't like it any more and I wanted to clean the motorhome after a week of being holed up. Most of all, I wanted to have a nice hot shower.

Every morning I would try the water supply tap outside to see if the pipe had thawed. I was so relieved on the morning I saw water running freely from the tap into my pan. I jumped for joy. It made me realise just how much I take water for granted and what a privilege it is to be able to get water from a tap.

Thankfully when the pipes thawed it was all good. There were no leaks. I had survived and managed – very well under the circumstances!

Chapter 13

Volunteering on the Farm

Throughout my journey over the last couple of years my aim has been to find myself and to be authentic; to be honest about what I want out of life so that women will relate to my journey and give them hope that they can enjoy old age. Things like the pandemic have thrown me a few curveballs and made me doubt what I was doing. But on the whole, I feel I have been moving forward.

I was feeling much braver and stronger within myself when I came across a page on Facebook called 'Work Exchange for Campers and Nomads'. It is a place where you can find work in exchange for free accommodation or hook-ups for motorhomes and campervans. As I glanced at the kind of things on offer, like looking after horses at a sanctuary in Greece or helping to build a place in Portugal, I spotted one that I thought was just up my street in Dorset, a county I knew very little about. A woman, who said she had a bad back, needed help for a couple of hours a day on her farm, in exchange for parking up a motorhome and free electricity. I was instantly drawn to it. I emailed her and waited to see what would happen next. It was exciting, the unknown. The next day I had a reply. Jan sounded lovely and asked me to tell her a bit more about myself and why I wanted to come. After several email exchanges we agreed that I would go and work there for a couple of weeks the following month. If it worked out for us both I could stay longer. If it wasn't what I thought it would be I could leave whenever I wanted. I had nothing to lose, and I felt that it was also time for me to test myself a bit more; to go outside my comfort zone – something I am encouraging other women to do.

The day I was due to drive down to Dorset, at the start of May, I was chatting to Sammy on the phone and she asked me, 'Where are you going? What are you going to be doing? Who are you going to be staying with?'

I replied, 'I'm not sure, but it will be exciting. I'll let you know when I get there.' She wasn't happy with my reply and insisted I pin drop her my location on WhatsApp the moment I got there. I wasn't sure how to do that but said that I would, thinking to myself, 'I'll work out how to do it when I get there.'

The drive to the farm was lovely. I didn't know Dorset at all and liked what I saw. I called into the pretty town of Sherborne on the way. Luckily I found the perfect parking spot on a side road. Normally I struggle to find places in small towns to pull in with the motorhome. The market was on and there was a busker on the street, which gave the place quite a vibrant feel. I wandered around and went in to explore the historic abbey. It was soon time for me to find the farm I was going to be working at.

I followed the main road out of Sherborne, past the turnoff for the castle and up the steep hill. I took a left turn and followed the narrow, winding road up the hill before stopping at the end of a driveway, not sure if it was the right place.

Suddenly I saw Jan waving at me from the top. She was very small and slim with long, grey hair hidden under a cap. She greeted me with such a warm smile and invited me in for a cup of tea. Straight away I thought she was pretty cool. I instantly wanted to know more about her. We chatted for ages, finding out more about each other. She then took me outside and showed me where I could park my motorhome. It was right next to the most glorious field of moon daisies that were in full bloom. I had never seen so many in one place. I drove around to the spot and parked up, noticing that there was a beautiful maple tree beside the van. It was the perfect setting. I couldn't believe my luck. She helped me get plugged into the electricity supply from the barn and showed me where I could get water and empty my toilet, then left me to settle in, saying, 'Please don't worry about working for the next couple of days, just get yourself settled into life here.'

I remembered that I had promised Sammy I would pin drop my location. I worked out how to do it and sent the message and also reassured her that Jan was lovely and that I thought I had landed on my feet here.

Jan had told me that she had been a single mother in a previous life and then met her husband, Lin. They fell in love, married and moved into this large property on fifteen acres of land. His mother was Dame Elisabeth Frink, a world-renowned sculptor and printmaker, who died in the early 1990s. He had lived a very privileged life, far removed from Jan's. She had been married before and done all kinds of jobs, from looking after horses and dogs to creating music and singing. She and Lin fell in love over music and formed their own little band to create their own. Sadly Lin died a few years ago. She told me with tears in her eyes how he was the love of her life and how painful it is being without him. She busies herself around the place, creating beautiful surroundings that she knows he would have loved. She still goes into her makeshift studio to create music, playing on her bass guitar and singing. I could see the lights on in the studio many times and I listened to the music filling the night air as I sat wrapped up on the step of my motorhome. I didn't want to intrude.

Jan would often invite me to join her for meals. We would listen to reggae and she would tell me about when they toured with their band over many years, to various music venues and festivals. I loved hearing all about her previous life. I even googled and found some of her old music, Boy le Monti. I thought it was brilliant and loved listening to it.

Since Lin died, Jan, who is in her late sixties, has run the place on her own. She sold the big house and converted one of the barns into a fab house for herself. It is so full of character: hats hanging on the walls, planks of wood hanging from chains for shelving, curtains made from old embroidered scarves. All add to her unique style.

Finally the day came for me to go out and earn my keep. I was a bit nervous as I had never done outdoor work and wasn't sure what I would be doing. Saying that, I was eager to get started. Jan gave me a quick tour and introduced me to the horses. We entered one stable and I thought the horse was dead. He was lying motionless on his side. Jan didn't seem bothered. Then I heard him snoring. It made us both laugh. Jan explained that Stanley, as he was called, was very lazy and loved to sleep. There was no rousing him until he was ready. I just had to video it because I had never seen a horse so sound asleep on his side like that. A few days later she washed his tail in a bucket of water and he didn't wake up throughout the whole procedure. You had to see it to believe it. She regularly took him out in a little trap along the country lanes. One day she let me ride alongside her. It was the first time I had ever been in one and I loved it.

Jan showed me the pink wheelbarrow and took me to the fields with the other horses in. She kept them outside most of the time because that is where they were happiest. They had shelter if the weather was bad but they could run free. They didn't wear horseshoes. Their hooves were regularly trimmed and maintained and they wore hoof boots when they were being ridden.

My first job was to collect the horse poo from the fields and deposit it on to a massive pile of manure in the corner of another field. Well, I loved it! The views, the fresh air, the sunshine, the exercise – all energised me. It was great fun. Thankfully the horse poo didn't smell like I thought it would. I filled my barrow numerous times and pushed it up and down the steep hills. I treated it like a good gym workout and it cost me nothing. When I finished poo collecting I went on to weeding around the edges of the fields where they were very overgrown. I loved that as well, pulling the long, winding weeds out from the bushes.

All the time I was working, I was building up my following on social media, engaging with women about what I was doing and how and why I had embarked on this lifestyle. I explained how I was facing yet another unknown. By coming to the farm I had unlocked things in me that I would not otherwise have done. I knew that by staying still I would not grow. With this in mind, once again I had gone outside my comfort zone, and I was the happier for it.

I think of the farm as my lucky place. After all the uncertainty of my life in my mid-fifties things finally started to come together during my stay there. The reason for my adventure became so much clearer. It wasn't about me but about what I could and would do for other women who are going through the same things I went through. They can see me coming out the other side with a renewed vigour for life. The catalyst was when I was contacted by a journalist who wanted to write a piece for the *Sunday Telegraph* about how we age differently after retirement nowadays. We are having more adventures. She had seen my Instagram feeds and liked my story. I was thrilled to be asked and agreed to be one of the 'retirement rebels' featured in the article. They sent a photographer to the farm to take pictures of me with my pink wheelbarrow collecting horse poo from the hills, which amused Serena and Celia, the other ladies caring for their horses at the place. They were as excited as I was that I was going to feature in a national newspaper. I had already been in several national magazines and on BBC Radio and had guest spots on several podcasts, but to me this was another level. Even the photographer, who had travelled all the way from London, said that he envied my lifestyle and it was his dream to be able to travel around and live in a motorhome. He said that he admired my courage.

When the article came out, we grabbed a copy from the post office a few miles down the road and rushed back to read it. I loved the picture they used of me. It was a half-page shot of me standing in the beautiful Dorset countryside, in front of my pink wheelbarrow full of horse poo, laughing my head off and enjoying life. It really did sum up how I was feeling about life in my retirement.

There was a great response to the article and more people contacted me to give talks. I felt a buzz about what I was doing. I had a feeling that the word was really beginning to get out there, challenging ageist stereotypes. I was being told more often that I was an inspiration to other women who would love to do what I am doing but cannot fathom a way of doing it. Even though I was doing it – living in my motorhome and having adventures – I still had the all-too-common feeling of imposter syndrome. In my head I had thoughts like, 'Who cares what I'm doing and what I say? Who am I to tell people how they can speak up and not accept ageist attitudes?' Well, the positive response and encouragement I got from people, including the girls on the farm, made me believe in myself more. I knew that my mission was to stop other women feeling broken and alone in their fifties like I had done, with no idea how they were going to live their lives as they aged. I was showing them by example that there is another way and it can be the route to happiness. The more comfortable I felt with myself and the more I believed that I could help women, the happier and stronger I became inside and with myself and my life.

Jan's daughter Rose came to visit for a few days from her place in Brighton. She asked if I wanted to go wild swimming in their local river, where she had been swimming since she was small. I jumped at the chance. She knew that area of the river well and knew that it was safe. She persuaded me to challenge myself and jump in from the high bridge: just another example of me facing a fear and overcoming it. As I jumped I shouted out, 'Say yes more!' to give myself Dutch courage. It was so exhilarating. I landed in the deep water below. It seemed like forever before I resurfaced, whooping out loud, 'Yeah I've done it!' Rose cheered me on from the side too, before jumping in to join me. We swam around in the river for ages, then it was time to get out. I presumed there would be somewhere I would be able to extricate myself with ease. That was not the case. The river banks were steep, very slippery and muddy. I had several failed attempts at getting out, as I just kept slipping back into the water. Rose showed me how to adopt what she called a 'monkey' position, using all four limbs to scramble up the bank. She made it look easy. I, on the other hand, didn't. I adopted the position but then did a mixture of digging my feet deep into the muddy banks of the river, then scrambling and rolling my body weight on to the grassy bank. It was hilarious. She filmed me and I put it on my social media and TikTok, where it has had thousands of views. It was a lesson in how not to climb out of a river.

We had such a good time by the river. It took me back to my carefree childhood days and I liked that feeling. I loved that Rose, in her thirties, didn't think twice about having a fun afternoon with a woman who was in her sixties. It just shows how intergenerational interactions are good for both age groups. This is exactly the kind of thing I mean when I tell women to revisit their childhood: swimming in rivers, rolling down hills, bike riding, etc. It reawakens feelings inside that make you feel happier about life and it challenges you and makes you feel more alive. It is all part of ageing positively. Small things can create ripples that become waves in our lives. It can make you see things differently and not accept the cards you feel you have been dealt. Do what feels right and good for you.

I stayed for several weeks enjoying life on the farm and the company of Jan and the other women, talking about what being old means to us. I loved that they challenged my views and gave me ideas about things. I am pleased that I took the risk to work on the farm. I did venture into the unknown and have subsequently made new friends and learnt a lot about myself along the way. I learnt that I love working outdoors, no matter what the weather, although it was mostly sunny during my time there. It was something I had never done in my life. I managed to lose my fear of horses by being around them more. I actually got back in the saddle and rode again for the first time in over forty years. It was something I loved when I was younger but never took with me into adult life. I did ache for days afterwards, though, after using muscles that had been dormant for so many years.

I kept saying how much I loved the outdoor work. All the other women said to me, 'Oh, you might not be saying that in the winter when it's raining all the time and the fields are all muddy.' I assured them that I would, and to prove it I said that I would be back at the end of the year for a few weeks, to experience it for myself.

On my last night there I sat up on a bench above the moon daisies with Jan. She lit a fire and I poured us a couple of gin and tonics. We chatted as we witnessed the most amazing blood red and orange sunset I have ever seen. She told me that when I first arrived she thought I seemed a little apprehensive but that she knew we would get along. She liked that I was doing what I wanted to do with my life. One of the things I love about Jan is that she seems such a free spirit. She just gets on with life and is so full of energy. She said that she was delighted things were happening for me. She knew that it was not all about me, but that I wanted to be a catalyst for changing attitudes; to be a support for women.

I asked her what she thought about getting old and she replied, 'As you get older you learn to know your mind. Things don't bother you so much. I think you should have as much fun as you can and learn to forgive.' I was with her wholeheartedly but am still working on the 'forgive' part.

It was sad saying goodbye because I had had such a positive experience.

* * *

True to my word, when November came around I headed back to Dorset. It was completely different. No fields of moon daisies to greet me as I drove up the drive but still the very warm welcome from Jan. I was so excited to be back that I didn't notice the grass was very soggy. As I tried to position my motorhome so that I got beautiful views over the fields, my front wheels got stuck in the mud. It was so stressful. They just kept spinning around. I tried to free it but I think I was just making the situation worse. Then Jan hopped into the driver's seat and tried to move it forward. It was still not going to budge. We tried putting straw and mats under the wheels … but it was going nowhere. Thankfully I knew I had a tow bar in a box under the passenger seat. As I got it out, Jan found the little hatch at the front passenger side of the motorhome and prised it open with a screwdriver. She screwed in the tow bar, then ran off and five minutes later came around the corner driving an enormous tractor and positioned herself so that she could tow me out. At first it didn't seem like that would work, then all of a sudden I got some traction and the motorhome moved forward and on to the driveway. It was a relief all round. I was slightly embarrassed that I had only been there for a few minutes and caused all this commotion. Jan is so laid back, though, she didn't care. I then got myself set up on some harder ground alongside the big barn. We used my long cable to connect me to the electricity supply inside the barn and I was all sorted. It was good to be back.

It had been raining a lot, so the fields and grounds were very muddy. I donned my waterproofs and sturdy walking boots to prepare me for the inclement weather. Nothing prepared me for just how hard it would be to push my wheelbarrow through the mud. I was slipping and sliding all over the place. But you know what? I was still smiling. I was still enjoying the experience. Over the few weeks I was there my leg muscles certainly got stronger and I found ways of manoeuvring the wheelbarrow along the sides of the field and walking backwards and forwards to empty the poop scoop into the barrow rather than pushing it around so much. Even when it rained I didn't mind. I would just have a nice hot shower when I had finished working.

I loved catching up with the girls on the farm again and even cooked lunch for us all one day. I loved hosting in Dora the Explora. They were impressed with my lifestyle and how cosy it was inside.

During my stay at the farm, life-changing things started to happen once again. I was contacted by a journalist from the *Guardian* for a column about starting out again over sixty. They sent a photographer out to take pictures of me. She was called Millie Pilkington, and it transpired that she had taken the private wedding photographs of the Duke and Duchess of Cambridge on their wedding day. Here she was clambering around my motorhome to get the best angles she could to take the photo. She said, 'I'm using a wide-angle lens as I must get your gin bar in', which made me laugh. She was absolutely lovely and very enthusiastic about what I was doing.

When the article came out I loved the picture they used of me, lounging in the motorhome in front of the gin bar. Straight away I began getting messages and emails from all over the world. People I hadn't heard from in years who lived in Australia messaged me to say they had read the article. The journalist contacted me a week later, saying that in the first four days over 900,000 people had read the article worldwide. I was blown away by the reaction to my lifestyle. I was thrilled that it was having such a positive response. I felt for so long that there was a lot being said about the menopause, and menopause in the workplace, but not enough about retired women over sixty. Who was speaking for us, to us, or about us? Now I was gaining a good platform to really get that conversation going. We do have a voice, we are not invisible and we do want this to be the best phase of our lives. Women contacting me from all over the world, especially those in their late fifties and sixties, said that they too would love to do what I am doing but they don't have the courage or the ability to do it. Many of them feel lost and angry with life. My social media went crazy. I felt a bit over-whelmed at first but tried to respond to as many as I could. I felt like an agony aunt to so many who really poured their hearts out to me about how difficult their work was, or how they were struggling through the menopause or just with their lives in general. They were looking to me for advice, but I could only tell them about my experiences and how I tackled things and faced fears.

In all the mayhem I got a funny message from my older brother, Paul, who I don't see very often as he has lived in Germany for many years, just saying, 'Remember I knew you before you were famous.' Then weeks later he sent me another message, telling me that someone had brought up my article in one of his night classes for a discussion about positive ageing. They thought I was a great example. They loved that I am a retirement rebel. I was thrilled that the article had stimulated such discussion. That is what I wanted to achieve.

After the initial feeling of being overwhelmed, I was ignited by the support I was getting. Every time I read the words 'you have inspired me', 'you are very brave' or 'what courage you have to do what you have done', it made me believe more in myself – and my message.

The opportunity to speak out was nearer at hand than I anticipated. Various TV channels and radio stations contacted me off the back of the newspaper article. Channel 5 News came down to the farm and filmed me. They broadcast a lovely piece that really captured what I was doing with my life in the van. Many local radio stations interviewed me. BBC Radio Solent even sent their breakfast reporter to the farm, at the crack of dawn. They interviewed me live several times.

Jan was brilliant. She could see that my world had gone a bit crazy and insisted I forget about doing any work for the time being as I was having to deal with all these media outlets. I was also asked to write articles for other magazines and *The i* newspaper. It felt good that at a time when I was feeling happier with my life, I was able to tell my story, of how I had felt broken in my fifties and struggled to cope with life, to now finding a pathway to happiness in my sixties. Around this time the

Women's Institute also put me on their list of inspirational speakers, which was a great boost. I was doing Zoom talks to very receptive women in the WI groups. They could relate to the struggles with work and the menopause and empty nest syndrome, when children grow up and leave home. It is a time when women often question the purpose of their lives: 'What now?' I am showing them a possible 'what now': overcoming fear and challenges; not self-limiting by thinking I can't do things. I am working out ways that I can do them. I loved the question and answer sessions after my talks. I really do get a warm feeling inside being able to help other women.

In the weeks that followed I got myself a literary agent and a book deal. It was a tremendous feeling. I cried because for the first time in my life I felt that people believed in me; that I had people in my corner who had my back. They wanted to listen to what I had to say. My opinion was valid. From leaving home when I was sixteen, I have had to fight all my own battles and make my way in life. Don't get me wrong, I have enjoyed the sense of achievement when I have come through hard times. I know I have not always got things right, but I didn't have anyone to teach me. I learnt from my mistakes. It is partly because of this that I have a lot of empathy for people trying to find their way in later life. We all need role models and people who have been there, done it, got the T-shirt. I want to be that role model and spokesperson for anyone who finds ageing a struggle.

During all this, I did go back to working for my keep on the farm. I enjoyed being outdoors and taking my mind off things for a few hours each day. It was great to have Jan around to talk to when I got overexcited about everything. She was a calming influence on me. She was a role model for me in the way she didn't let things stress her out. When I had interviews or had to submit articles she understood, and encouraged me to focus on that, saying that I could work when I had finished.

During my last week on the farm, Jan organised one of her infamous reggae nights that I had been hearing about. She hosts them in her barn. I helped her decorate it with candles hung up on massive iron chandeliers, she erected special atmospheric lighting and we arranged sofas, chairs and tables. The invites were extended to friends and some locals, and around thirty people came. It was an entertaining evening. Jan was the DJ. She called herself DJ Incompetence … not to be confused with incontinence. She made everyone laugh because she needed her glasses and a special light, and at times a magnifying glass as well, to ensure she got the stylus on the vinyl record. Often it would whirr in, or jump, but it made us all laugh and added to the craziness of the night. The average age of the attendees was around sixty. It was great to see everyone just up and dancing all night. I loved the feeling of freedom. What a fabulous way to end my stay on the farm. I will be back.

Chapter 14
I Was Ready for
My Dream to Come True

The time had come for me to realise my dream and head off to the Outer Hebrides. It felt like the right time as I was in a much better place, both psychologically and physically, than when I had embarked on my retirement. On my journey over the last few years I have found calmness and stillness in my life. I have found a place to breathe. I have allowed myself at every opportunity the space and time to get to know people and places and to learn from them. It has been life-changing for me.

So with this in my heart, I was so excited to be travelling to the place I had dreamt about for so long. I had hoped to visit at the start of my travels in Dora the Explora, but Covid put paid to that. To be honest, in hindsight it was a good thing because I was too messed up emotionally then to have taken on board what I envisaged the islands had to offer me.

When I arrived at my friend Ged's house in Glasgow, she asked if she could possibly join me on the first couple of nights in the Outer Hebrides. She would then get a ferry back on her own. I thought it would be fun to kickstart my adventure with a girls' road trip. Besides, Ged had been to the islands before. She would be able to show me some special places that I might otherwise have missed.

Throughout my life I have hated that feeling when you are late for planes, ferries, etc. So I told her it was to be a very early start to ensure we didn't miss the ferry at Oban, as this was my dream trip.

My alarm went off at 6 a.m. I jumped out of bed full of excitement, like a kid at Christmas. It was the day I was finally off to the Outer Hebrides. It didn't take me long to pack up the motorhome and secure everything so it wouldn't fly around as I drove along. As good as her word, Ged was ready to go at 6.30. It was a beautiful drive past the shores of Loch Lomond, where we stopped at an amazing viewing point to take pictures. Low clouds and snow-capped mountains in the distance added to the magical, early morning feel of the drive. When we got to Oban, I grabbed us a couple of croissants for breakfast from the supermarket … okay, and another few bottles of wine for later! We had hours before the ferry, so we drove to a lovely beach just outside the town. It was chilly, but the sun was out so we wrapped up warm, put the table and chairs out and settled down to eat our croissants with a cup of coffee. We chatted with the early morning dog walkers passing by, who were amused at our set-up.

We eventually packed up and headed for the port, where we had time to sit out again in the sunshine with a brew. For me this is all part of the fun. I love to take my time and not feel rushed or pressurised.

I posted a video on social media because I was so excited to be realising my dream. My phone rang shortly afterwards and it was Sammy. 'I'm not happy' was her first statement, then she went on to say, 'Will you please stop telling people where you're going and where you are now and when you'll be alone?'

In my video I had said when Ged would be heading back on the ferry, which showed that I would then be alone again. I had previously agreed with Sammy that I would only post on social media once I had left a place, for safety reasons. In my excitement this morning I had forgotten our agreement and just blurted out what I was doing. I apologised and said I would be more vigilant from now on.

The ferry crossing took nearly six hours. I wrapped up warm in a thick hooded coat, hat, scarf, gloves and sunglasses. I wanted to be on deck to take in everything. I didn't want to miss a thing. I was blown away by the beauty of the islands and the scenery as we sailed by. I loved the way the sea colours changed as the sunlight hit the water and shimmered in the distance. I felt like bursting. I was so happy and I had not even set foot yet on the first island. Ged, unfortunately, was feeling pretty queasy most of the trip and kept herself to herself.

Out on deck I got to witness the most spectacular sunset. The reds and oranges filling the sky were so vibrant.

As we drove off the ferry I gave a little squeal because I was on the Isle of Barra. It was very dark. We drove along the single-track road in the pitch black. When we eventually arrived at the Wavecrest campsite we couldn't tell where to park, and there was no one around. It just looked like a big patch of grass. I couldn't see if it was okay for me to park on in the dark. If it was too wet I would get stuck straight away and would need a tractor to pull me out.

I began to panic a bit as I was on a single-track road in the dark with no idea what to do. I called the phone number on the sign. A very friendly woman called Margaret Mary answered and apologised for not being there but said she would be over in five minutes. I saw her approaching with her torch in hand. I excitedly explained that I was worried about where to park. She walked me over to the best place and showed me where the electric hook-up was and left us to it. We were soon set up and cooking dinner. I made spicy chicken, new potatoes and broccoli. We had a glass of wine and then settled down for the night. I was beyond excited about the prospect of waking up in the morning and seeing where we were located. I could hear the roar of the sea but couldn't make out anything else.

I woke at daylight to the sound of the ocean. I grabbed my phone and started a video to capture the moment I saw where we were parked up. I am so glad I did because what I saw when I opened the door exceeded my expectations. In the video you can hear the emotion in my voice as I see just how close we are to the rugged coastline and dark blue sea. I just cried with sheer joy. We sat outside with our morning coffee and absorbed the wonder of it all. I could never have imagined it would be this beautiful, even when reading about it all these years.

Ged wanted me to see the neighbouring island of Vatersay, the southernmost inhabited island in the Outer Hebrides, which was connected to Barra by a causeway in 1991. It is the start of the Hebridean Way long-distance walking and cycling routes, which end in Lewis, some ten islands later.

I was definitely wowed. It is a beautiful island, with lots of sand dunes. We ventured down on to the east beach first. I was stunned by the turquoise water and the beautiful, unspoilt, long, white, sandy beach. There was no one else around. I just had to run back to the motorhome and change into my costume. As I submerged myself into the the Sea of the Hebrides, I took a sharp intake of breath as – you've guessed it – it was pretty cold, but so exhilarating. I swam around for about a minute then ran out with my body tingling, feeling so happy. The sun was actually quite warm on my back as I put on my towelling robe and my thick coat.

I stood and looked at the turquoise sea and pale sands that went on for miles. It just looked like somewhere exotic; the freezing-cold water was a reality check that it wasn't. It was a cold March in the Outer Hebrides. In that moment I was so conscious that I was living the life I wanted to live. Nothing was stopping me doing crazy things like submerging myself in icy-cold waters on a winter's day in the Outer Hebrides. It is only a small thing, I know, but it gave me a feeling of being brave and strong. I was not letting fear limit me. I really felt that I had come out of the wreckage of the menopause and my mid-fifties and was more open to challenging myself on every level, and I liked that feeling.

Ged had a quick dip in the icy waters before we went back to the motorhome and had a hot drink and a sandwich.

We accessed the beach on the west side over the machair. What we saw was in complete contrast to the calm east beach. Here the big Atlantic waves were crashing on to the pristine white sands, but there were a lot more pebbles too. We sat for ages looking out to sea, chatting about how unspoilt the place was and how lucky we were to be visiting with no one around.

We had heard that the Northern Lights might be visible so later on we wrapped ourselves in blankets and sat outside to see if we could see them.

They were very subtle. At first we were asking each other, 'Is that them? Do you think that's them starting?' Then they began to take shape: the green light dancing around the sky, with a reddish tint to it. Ged got some great pictures. It was wonderful to share the excitement of the moment. I cried because it was just the icing on the cake. My lifetime dreams coming true.

* * *

Barra airport is famous for being the only airport in the world where scheduled flights use a tidal beach as a runway. I just had to see this for myself. Ged and I drove around the spectacular scenery of the island to a good vantage point. We could see this little speck in the distance approaching the sands. It was exciting to see it eventually land and taxi to the little terminal where the passengers alighted. Something I will be adding to my bucket list before I am seventy is flying to and landing on Barra in a small plane.

I dropped Ged off at the ferry port at six the following morning. I was sad to see her go, but also up for exploring the islands on my own. I sat outside to have my breakfast overlooking the blustery sea. My heart was full. It was everything I had wanted and more. I would never forget this place – my first experience on these special islands.

I had a new neighbour in a campervan: Francis and his dog, Piper. We went walking in the hills. He had a handy little app that showed the routes. I am useless at following maps so it was nice to have someone lead the way. I tend to just set off in one direction and see what I can find. Initially we got lost, but once we realised our error, we headed off in the right direction.

It was quite wet underfoot and hard going at first, making our way up the steep hill over heather and peat hags. I started out puffing and panting like an old steam engine and my knee was pretty painful, but I soldiered on. Francis was very chilled. He was happy to go at my pace. After half an hour I got into my stride and felt quite lively. The surrounding hills were beautiful and we got some exhilarating views as we sat and had lunch. Francis converts vehicles to run on cooking fat, which I found amazing. He asks for fat at pubs and shops for his van. They are happy to give it to him because they would otherwise have to pay to get rid of it.

Trust me to arrive on Barra as they were expecting extremely high winds. Margaret Mary said, 'If it gets too bad we can put you in the barn', which gave me some indication they were a bit concerned. Her husband, Douglas, checked that I would be okay and advised me to check which direction the wind was going to hit and to move my van to point it into the wind. Francis then tucked his van in behind mine, which gave him a bit of protection. The winds on the first night reached sixty-six miles per hour, which was very rocky; fun but also a bit scary … I did have thoughts of 'What if it does actually blow over?'

Over the next couple of days we pooled food and cooked and ate together. We also went for some lovely walks in the high winds, before he headed off on his adventure and I was once again alone.

Another advantage of living my carefree existence is being able to take up kind invitations at the drop of a hat. A woman who follows me on social media and who was holidaying on Barra asked me if I wanted to have dinner with her and her husband. It was nice to get the invite out of the blue. When I pulled up outside their holiday home I was both nervous and excited. I had absolutely no idea what they would be like, but I already knew that I liked them for extending a hand of friendship.

We had a fabulous evening eating bangers and mash and talking about our lives. I felt relaxed in their company almost immediately. Stefan, who is from Germany, and Teresa, who is English and a life coach, were the type of people that fill your soul and make you feel good about life.

I left them feeling very happy and saying we would all go to the pub on the Friday night. Sadly we didn't get to do that, as they had gone on a day ferry trip to Eriskay but due to high winds they got stranded there. The ferry stopped running.

Once the wind died down, I went for another amazing swim on Vatersay. Afterwards I was walking along the beach when I got talking to two ladies from Cheshire. They thought I was brave going into the water. We had a lovely chat and they kindly took photographs for me. They said they would look me up on social media and promised to look out for my book when it came out. Once again I left the beach feeling so invigorated and buoyed up by an interaction with women around my age. They kept saying, 'We get it': that feeling of getting old and making sense of life. Their pleasure at seeing what I was doing and how I was living my life fuelled my soul. It made me even more determined to help other women feel this positive about life.

As I waited for the ferry from Barra to Eriskay I bought a bacon buttie from a great little cafe at the ferry port. The couple who ran it had moved to the island a few weeks before after travelling in their van. They wanted to know about my travels and wished me luck living in my motorhome.

I was excited and nervous about driving on to the ferry because it was very small. As I stepped out of the van I was greeted by a smiley Australian woman, who I later found out was called Heather, and her travelling companion, Carol. Apparently the couple in the cafe had told them about me and they were intrigued. We spent the ferry crossing swapping stories about how we all help women get the best out of life: Heather through mentoring and art, Carol through mentoring as well. They said they had booked a table to have dinner at the Am Politician pub and did I want to join them?

I drove off the ferry and headed straight to the Am Politician. I knew it was famous for being named after a ship that sank with thousands of bottles of whisky on board; islanders salvaged much of the cargo. It inspired the film *Whisky Galore!*

I bumped into the women from Cheshire I had encountered at Vatersay Bay again and we had a coffee and a natter. The women asked me lots of questions about my life in the van. Hearing myself telling them what I had been up to in the last few years made me feel proud of what I had achieved. They were impressed that I had recently been in *Yorkshire Life* magazine, which they said they subscribed to, vowing to go back home and seek out the article to read.

We asked the landlady about the pub's history and she showed us some bottles of whisky retrieved from the vessel, a shot gun and some money, laying them out on the bar for us to photograph. I took the opportunity to mention I would be eating there that night and asked if I could park overnight. The landlady was only too pleased to show me a parking spot beside the pub and said that at this time of year, with so few tourists, no one would mind – my first, sort of, wild camp.

Dinner with the Australians was such fun. We ended up drinking shots and having such a laugh. It was nice to be 'out out'. We even had some friendly banter with the locals who were enjoying their Saturday night out.

With a bit of a thick head the next morning I explored Eriskay along the single-track roads. It is only three miles long and one and a half miles wide, with a population of less than 150. I kept thinking to myself, 'Oh, I wonder where that road goes', and finding some magical spots, or old derelict buildings that I just had to photograph. It saddens me that so many of the historic houses have been left to get so dilapidated. My imagination runs wild and I think of the people who dwelt in those old cottages and what kind of lives they would have had on these blustery islands. I totally lost myself and all track of time in the beauty of my surroundings. I did a quick shop at the local grocery store, grabbing fresh fruit and veg and a few things like a ball of string and clear tape – not that I necessarily needed it, but I felt it would be useful in case of emergencies. Things were slightly more expensive but I wanted to shop local and support the local economy.

I drove over the causeway from Eriskay to South Uist, where I stayed for a couple of nights at the Kilbride campsite. There was a beautiful, rugged beach and hills to walk along over the road, so I went off exploring in the strong winds. It is at times like this that I loved my own company, wandering aimlessly and exploring. It was so liberating meandering over the soggy ground with the roar of the sea on one side and the wind almost blowing me off my feet.

The site owner, Donald, checked that I had positioned my motorhome correctly, as they were predicting very high winds again and he wanted to make sure I was safe. I liked how kind the islanders were, wanting the best for you. They always seemed to have time for a nice chat and didn't seem to be in a rush – a far cry from the life I had been living before my retirement.

Once again mine was the only motorhome on the site. I had the run of the facilities and did all my washing in the washing machine. And had long, hot showers.

One day my Australian friends came to see me. It was exciting to get visitors. I made us a brew then we went for a walk on the hills. I loved their positive energy. They were all about women supporting women. We compared notes about midlife scenarios for many women and agreed that it is the same the world over. It is vital we have a voice and do not accept that life will pass us by as we get older. We need to support one another to go for it, not knowing how long we will live for. Things are changing for older women and we all play our part to help each other with that change, to feel more positive about our goals in life and not settle and self-limit, but to strive for a purpose.

It was time for me to push myself a bit more by doing a spot of wild camping. I drove for ages, following a single-track road trying to find the perfect wild camping place. I got frustrated because all the times I wasn't looking, I saw some perfect locations where I thought to myself, 'That would be a great little spot to camp.' Now I was looking, there was nowhere suitable.

Just as I was about to give up, a car going in the opposite direction pulled up in a passing place to let me past. I slowed down and asked the driver if he knew of anywhere I could wild camp. I wasn't sure if he would snap at me that I shouldn't even be contemplating wild camping in the first place. I was lucky. He smiled and told me his name was Simon Davies and he did guided walks in the wild. He handed me one of his leaflets then told me to follow him back the way I had already come for a few miles. When he stopped at his house I was to take the next left then follow the road for a couple of miles where I would find the perfect area to park up. He wasn't wrong … it was beyond perfect for my first spot of wild camping. There was no WiFi or phone signal, which just added to the feeling of joy. I totally switched off and watched birds of prey flying overhead and the wild ponies just wandering past the motorhome along the road to who knows where.

The sunset was entrancing. All the rusty colours of the hills in front of me changed as the sun set. To add to the magical feel, there was a full moon that lit up the sky. I pulled a blanket around me and just wandered about looking up at the wonderful stars, making out the different constellations like Orion's Belt or The Plough. I don't have the words to express what I was feeling. It was out of this world. It was perfect wild camping, in total silence, something I often crave but rarely get to experience: just switching off from everything and everybody. I had one of the best nights' sleep I had had in ages. This place just kept on giving. The following morning when I opened my door, the colour scheme on the hills was different again as the sunlight reflected off the peaks. The rusty reds, browns and mustard tones all mixed together to create the perfect backdrop. I made a coffee and wandered around taking in the beauty of it all. I felt a great sense of achievement that I had had my first proper wild camp at sixty-two years old and thoroughly enjoyed it. There was an honesty box by the car park. I put some money in to pay for the privilege of camping in such amazing surroundings.

The weather then took a turn for the worse: the skies went dark grey and the heavens opened. The rain was bucketing down as I packed up the van to head to North Uist. It didn't dampen my spirits, though. I was now a convert to wild camping. It is crazy just how quickly the weather changes: the sun was trying to break through, even though it was still raining, as I drove along the road. I was then stopped in my tracks: right in front of me was the most perfect full rainbow that I have ever seen in my life. It blew me away. I jumped out of the van – getting soaked, but I didn't care – to take photographs of it. I felt no one would believe me if I didn't take a picture. It was just too perfect. Then, as if by magic, there was a second slightly more blurred rainbow. This was very significant to me and I cried with happiness.

After I had got rid of all my negative emotions by Loch Morlich near Aviemore, when I was feeling broken and scared at the start of my journey nearly two and a half years ago, the amazing double rainbow I had seen as I drove away had made me cry because it somehow signified to me that things were going to be okay. I was taking control of my life, leaving behind the negativity and looking forward with courage.

Now here I was seeing the most perfect double rainbow, feeling like a completely different woman. I had ventured out of my comfort zone on my explorations in Dora the Explora and become the woman I always felt I should be. I had been prevented from fulfilling my potential by so many knockbacks and by circumstances in my life. I now felt strong and able to have a voice. When I clambered back into the motorhome, dripping wet, it was one of the only times that I truly wished I had someone alongside me to share this experience with. It was pure joy.

I wanted to check out the Pobull Fhinn stone circle on North Uist. As I parked up my motorhome and looked to my right, a car had pulled up alongside me. I thought, 'That's pretty close', then I saw this big smile. It was Heather, the Australian woman I had met on the ferry. We squealed with delight that we had met up again. What are the chances of that? She was just heading off to Taigh Chearsabhagh Museum and Arts Centre and asked if I wanted to hop in and go along with her. There was a fabulous exhibition about the history of the island and some of the smaller surrounding islands.

We then went on a very long walk to the stones in the afternoon, getting lost along the way but experiencing the most wonderful views across the hills. Once again we had extremes of weather in a matter of hours: rain, sleet, sunshine and very high winds that nearly blew us off our feet. I loved it. It was so exhilarating. Back at Heather and Carol's nice hotel, I asked if I could park overnight if I joined the girls for dinner in the restaurant. They said yes and I got to fill my water container and charge my phone and laptop.

* * *

Driving to the Isle of Berneray over the causeway was beautiful. I was excited to meet Eilidh, the woman who runs the Coralbox Gift Shop on the island. I had followed her on Instagram for a long time, admiring her photographs of the Outer Hebrides as I planned my dream trip. Now I was going to meet up with her. She was getting her shop ready to reopen for the season as I pulled up. She was as lovely as I hoped she would be. I bought myself a ring from her shop to remember my trip on the islands.

Then I said that I would head off to explore and maybe we could go for a walk a bit later when she had finished her jobs.

I headed off to the beaches, including West Beach, which runs the entire length of the island. I drove up on the hills. I was conscious that it had been raining heavily over the last few days so the grass would be soggy. With this in mind I drove very tentatively along the single track, only to see it come to a dead end at a cemetery. I knew I had to turn around and there really wasn't much room to manoeuvre. I gave it a go. Unfortunately one of my tyres went on to the grass and got well and truly stuck. I felt sick in the pit of my stomach.

I remembered that my brother Paddy told me not to use the accelerator, as this would only make matters worse. He taught me to use the clutch alone to try to free myself. I tried this for ages but it was not moving. I even got out and tried to push the motorhome, which made me laugh out loud as there was not a chance I could make it budge anywhere. I got the mats out and tried pushing them under the wheel to get traction. No luck. I called my roadside assistance, only to be told I'm not covered for something like this. I would have to call a recovery service to pull me out.

I felt lost. I texted Eilidh and explained that I would not be going for a walk anywhere as I was currently lodged in the ground on the hilltop. She said there may be some crofters down the road and she would send her friend Jenny to help.

I decided to have another go at the clutch technique. I turned the key in the ignition to set the engine running and gently lifted the clutch and released it, keeping my foot well away from the brake or accelerator. This created a tiny rocking motion of the tyre. It went a fraction backwards and forwards each time.

I did this for about fifteen, twenty minutes, very, very gently. All of a sudden I got a sense that the tyre was getting a tiny bit of traction. Very slowly it edged forward, tiny bit by tiny bit. I hardly dared hope that I was actually going to do this and free myself, then lo and behold it moved forward off the grass. I was out of the ditch. I was ecstatic.

I took lots of pictures of the ditch to show my brother how I had got myself free thanks to his advice. I was so proud that I had managed to stay calm. Before I would have just lost the plot and cried and been useless, but I had stuck with it and done the job. It is amazing what you can do if you push your limits.

I was still not out of the woods, though, because I was still facing in the wrong direction.

Jenny arrived with her smaller campervan and calmly guided me into the cemetery area, where the ground was a bit firmer. I was able to turn around and head off. After all that I was just mentally exhausted and didn't feel like going for a walk. I explained this to Eilidh and she totally understood.

I drove off and found a lovely little place to wild camp for the night and thought about what I had actually achieved that day. I was so pleased with myself.

I loved everything about the isles of Lewis and Harris; their contrasting styles.

A visit to the Calanais Standing Stones on Lewis was a highlight. They are one of Scotland's oldest man-made structures. There are several groupings of them dotted around the island. I don't know why, but when I visited the Calanais III group of stones I felt really empowered. I walked to the top of the hill and instinctively outstretched my arms. At the same time in my head I heard the words, 'I am back, I told you I would be back, I am a warrior.' I cried and my legs felt weak. It was symbolic for me: the revelation of who I am ... 'a warrior' ...

This was my true beginning. I had had to go through the last few years finding my authentic self. Now I could embark on the best phase of my life on my terms. It was a very powerful and forceful emotion. I have to know who I am to be able to connect and communicate effectively in my life. I feel these last few years on the road in my motorhome have helped me find who I am. I have spent too many years trying to gain the approval of people who quite honestly I didn't even like. I judged my self-worth by their opinion of me, even though I didn't respect them as people. I saw them as having some kind of power over my life. That is madness now that I look back. I know there are many women in similar situations. I know now that I am finding a better, healthier future for me both mentally and physically. I have peace in my heart. I hope I can help other women find that inner belief and peace.

* * *

The beaches on the west coast of Lewis are fabulous. Uig Sands is vast, but my favourite was Reef Beach. I had spent several nights wild camping and desperately needed to charge my batteries. I also needed to submit another chapter of my book to the publishers. But there were no campsites open.

Getting desperate for electricity, I called a site on Reef Beach. A chap called Finn answered and said they were closed. I begged him to let me stay. He then gave me a dressing-down saying, 'Did you not check if the sites were open before you came to the island? Why did you come if you knew they were closed?'

I explained that I live in my van and was working my way up the islands. Eventually he relented a bit and said, 'Well, what time can you get here?' I asked what would suit him. He replied that he had to go to the shop for five minutes so I should get myself there by half two and he would see what he could do. I think he wanted to check out who this pushy woman was on the other end of the phone. I realised on this trip that if I want to wild camp regularly, I need to invest in some solar panels to generate my own electricity to charge up my phone and laptop.

It was the most spectacular drive through rugged terrain to the site. I stopped and asked a couple who had luxury pods where the site was. When I heard the man talk I asked if he was from Yorkshire. He laughed and recoiled and said, 'Manchester, the right side of the Pennines.' We both laughed and I said, 'I suppose you're going to give me the wrong directions now because I insulted you ... ' He laughed and pretended to do just that. He said that the campsite was shut, though. I told him that I had had a chat on the phone with Finn and hopefully he was going to let me stay. He said, 'Oh, he's a good man, Finn, he'll help you. He is King. Just make him a cup of coffee.' With that tip I headed off up the steep single-track road and around a sharp corner ... What I saw just blew me away: the white, sandy beach that went on for ages and the beautiful turquoise sea that glistened as the light hit it. I have seen some wonderful beaches, but this jumped to the top of my favourites list. I had not bargained for this ... I was just in search of electric hook-up. This was such a bonus.

Finn was waiting to greet me. He had a very friendly, lived-in face with a white beard. He shook my hand and chatted away to me, telling me that the site didn't open until May. I felt pretty soon that he had decided he liked me and was going to help me. The car park was full of people who were taking advantage of the good weather and had gone for a walk on the beach, so he told me to hang fire and as soon as someone drove off I could reverse into their slot and park up for the night and he would switch one of the electricity supplies on especially for me. I gave him some money and thanked him and told him he was a lifesaver. I told him I would make him the best cup of coffee ever the moment I was plugged in.

Not long afterwards I reversed into position. I gave him the electric cable to plug in. He climbed over the fence and down the hill to the electric point and fumbled about a bit before coming back laughing at me, saying I'd given him the wrong end. When we got it all plugged in and I checked inside my heart sank: the electricity supply light wasn't on. He looked worried and said, 'Wait a minute, I'll go and try another switch.' When he emerged the supply worked and we were both happy. As promised, I made us both a cup of coffee and we sat outside at the bench table in the sunshine.

He was so lovely to chat to. He told me he was born in Reef and his first language was Gaelic. He bemoaned the fact that fewer people were learning the language. He told me about living in London for ten years working on the buses. He would never go back, it was too fast for him. He said he found it hard that no one spoke to him when he first arrived there, because back home on Lewis, where he grew up, everyone chatted and was friendly.

He had also travelled a lot around the world and had some interesting tales to tell. I could have talked to him for hours. He checked that I was settled and said he would see me the next day.

The next morning the peace and quiet was broken by men doing coastal erosion work, trying to stem the tides of time: the coast in this particular part of the island is receding at about ten feet a year according to Finn.

I climbed the hill across the road from the site. That was the only place I could get a good signal and I wanted to send another book chapter to my publisher and do some Zoom calls. Afterwards I stayed up there, lying in the winter sunshine, wrapped up in my hat and big scarf, loving the feeling of the warmth of the sun on my face as I gazed up at the clouds. I have always loved doing that, ever since I was a youngster. I feel calm and peaceful just lying down looking up at the sky. It was wonderful to have the time to do that once again in my life.

Finn visited again in the late afternoon. I made us coffee and we chatted about Scottish music and bands that he liked to listen to. He said he liked a lot of country music, which he bought when he was travelling in America. He certainly has lived an interesting life. He said he only volunteered to help look after the site for the community for a year ... five years later he was still doing it. He admitted, though, that he loved it because he met all kinds of people from all over the world, many becoming friends as they came back every year with their families. He pointed out several good walks for me to do in the area and I said I would do them the next day.

I wanted to do the walk Finn told me about where some local lads had erected a cross on the top of the hill. I was intrigued. He reassured me that it looked far steeper than it actually was when you got up close, so I would be able to ascend it with no trouble.

I trudged over the sand dunes and through the very boggy fields and began the climb. I'm not sure that my idea of steep is the same as Finn's. I found it pretty hairy in parts, but I was determined to get to the top. I would figure out how to get down when I was up there. It was well worth the climb. The cross was made from local stone and looked striking jutting out of the summit. The views were wonderful.

Eventually it was time to descend. Easier said than done. My legs always get a bit wobbly when I am uncertain of a route down, which is not always helpful. I tentatively picked my way down the steep hill, falling on to my bottom and shuffling a bit when it was too difficult; grabbing on to handfuls of heather and rocks that jutted out. I got a bit too cocky, though, and before I knew it I slid on a particularly boggy bit and my left leg buckled and tucked behind me. The pain just radiated up my leg and for a second I thought I might have broken something. I stayed still for a few minutes just focusing on my breathing then moved my leg and thankfully it was okay, just tender. When I got to the bottom I checked again and all was okay. It did make me realise, though, that things can change in a second, and that I needed to install the what3words app on my phone, like my brother Paddy had been nagging me to do, so that should anything happen, the emergency services would know where I was.

I carried on walking over the hills in the other direction to a beautiful loch. I plonked myself down and just stared. Wow, yet another breathtaking vista. These islands were magical. I ate some nuts and an apple and had a drink. Then I just lay on my back and listened to the water lapping on the rocks for nearly an hour. It was glorious. I didn't have to be anywhere. I did try to meditate, but my head was too full of thoughts and wouldn't let me. But it was still very relaxing.

I was glad to get back to the motorhome. Nearly four hours of walking on very boggy terrain up and down hills with a dodgy knee had taken it out of me. All I wanted was a nice cup of tea.

As much as I loved Reef Beach, it was time to move on. I wrote a letter to Finn thanking him for opening up his heart and the campsite to me. I told him how much I had loved his company and wished him well for the season.

As I was deciding where to go next, I got a message from my Aussie friend Heather, saying that the woman who ran the darkroom where she had an artist's residency had kindly said that I could park up there for a couple of nights. Only a few years ago, I didn't feel worthy of this level of kindness and goodness. But this trip has changed my mindset: if good things happen to me, it is because I deserve it.

I drove to Stornoway and wandered around Lews Castle and the museum, which gave me a strong feeling of community among the people in the Outer Hebrides.

I arrived at the little bothy where Heather was staying and parked up. It was nice to hook up to electricity again. She was busy doing her photography work in the darkroom all morning. I spent hours writing. In the afternoon we drove to the Bridge to Nowhere. When I saw the name on the map, I knew I just had to find out more about the place. We parked up and walked over the bridge, which is sometimes called the Garry Bridge because it spans the beautiful gorge overlooking Garry Beach. It was originally intended to be part of a route to Ness, but now it really is a bridge to nowhere. We walked over it and along a dirt track along the cliffs, to the point where the pathway just peters out.

I was so glad that we had gone in Heather's car because the last bit of the road was very narrow and winding. My heart was in my mouth a couple of times. I know I would never have been able to navigate that road in the motorhome. I do know my limitations.

I liked hanging out with Heather, as we had some great conversations. She was always telling me to stop saying sorry. I didn't realise just how often I say it until she pointed it out. I need to stop apologising for my existence. I am working on it.

After I left Heather, the last week of my Outer Hebrides experience was exploring Harris. Of course I headed for the Harris Distillery and came away with a nice bottle of their gin to grace my motorhome gin bar. I got myself a little bag from the Harris Tweed Company. I explored several beaches. Heather surprised me again by driving down from Stornoway for the day to join me beach-hopping. I even got her to have a spontaneous dip in the very chilly Atlantic in our pants and T-shirts.

My last night on Harris was spent wild camping in the atmospheric hills just outside Tarbert, on the road to Stornoway, in a storm. The winds buffeted the motorhome. I had to drive to the port at six o'clock in the morning in the pitch black, heavy rain and high winds. I admit I did feel a bit scared but also pleased with myself that I didn't let that stop me from having this awesome experience.

I was on such a high when I got off the ferry on the Isle of Skye, having just lived my dream for over a month. I made the long, scenic drive to Glasgow to stay overnight with a friend and was still on cloud nine when I drove to Leeds the following day, to see family. It was then that I was brought down to earth with a bump. Literally. I was tired from all the driving and I hit a wall reversing. All three back bits of the motorhome were cracked and hanging off, including the registration plate. I was so cross with myself. I taped them up as best I could with some clear tape I had bought at the little shop on Eriskay, in case of emergencies, and set off at the crack of dawn to drive to Kent, where I was due to house-sit. On the motorway a lorry flashed its lights at me, to let me know that my rear end was hanging off. I pulled on to the hard shoulder of a slip road and tied it up with the ball of string that I also got in the Eriskay shop, for emergencies. Thank goodness I did. I don't know what I would have done otherwise. I managed to drive for six hours, very slowly, down to Kent, stopping regularly at service stations to check it was all still safe and adding extra string where necessary.

This is a good example of life throwing things at us when we least expect it. For years I felt I couldn't deal with problems. Now that I feel so differently about myself in my sixties, as a consequence I am able to face things head on and work out solutions. It empowers me. I am no longer a victim of what life throws at me. Yes this was a bad day, but it only made me realise that I am a strong, brave woman and that as women we all have courage; it's just a case of finding it.

Chapter 15

What I Have Learnt and What Next

When I first had my crazy idea to downsize my life and hit the road, I could not have envisaged the impact it would have on me as a woman. I remember how scared I was leaving my flat and setting off in a big van with my few possessions in it, not really knowing what life had in store for me but more determined than ever to be mistress of my own destiny, wherever it took me.

Slowly, bit by bit as I embraced my motorhome life, I could see the wood for the trees. I began to realise what I would and would not accept in my life. I reached out to other women and shared stories. This gave me fire in my belly to help change things for them. I gave talks to women's groups and often they would approach me afterwards in tears because my story was so relatable. My life had become horrible in my mid-fifties, and I thought I was alone and hid from family and friends. I hope by telling my story women will begin to open up about their problems and this in turn will bring about change. For many years women have struggled with the menopause in the workplace. Now things are changing and many workplaces are taking steps to introduce policies that make life better for staff who are menopausal.

After three years of travelling Great Britain in my motorhome and championing positive ageing by speaking and writing about it, I am a completely different person. I cannot believe I ever let myself get so lost in my life, because now I feel like a warrior with a mission to continue capitalising on life's lessons that I have learnt along the way.

I have learnt that I can be strong when I need to be, but it is also okay to ask for help and guidance when I am unsure. I do not have to do things alone. There is a wonderful tribe of women out there who support one another, and there is nothing more powerful than that.

I have found my voice. When I say yes I mean yes; when I say no I mean no. And it is okay to say no to things you do not want to do in life.

I realise that for years I was a people-pleaser, to the exclusion of my own happiness and needs. Not any more. As a consequence, I am a far more relaxed person to be around. I am in a better frame of mind to help others and offer kindness.

I realise that I have faced many fears in my life and overcome them. It was important for me to tell my story because I can only talk from my own experiences, both good and bad. I wanted to show that I have been on a rollercoaster of emotions and situations in my life and battled through them to my happy place. I want my story to inspire and help as many women as possible.

My advice to young women is to challenge anti-ageing attitudes. Insist on pro-ageing not anti-ageing products, which just play on people's insecurities about getting older. Look around you to see how your older female colleagues are being treated. Would you want that to happen to you? What can you do to improve the situation for when you are the older team member? What policies can you help to introduce? How can you help change the narratives around ageing?

To older women I would say, you are enough. Your voice is valid. You do not have to accept ageist attitudes or bullying behaviour. Old is good, and you are never too old for adventure. Do not kill your potential to have the life you deserve. Do not let fear keep you from doing the things that you want to do. You can fulfil your dreams.

My goal is to be a spokeswoman for older women to help them find a way to age that makes them truly happy and to not be afraid of ageing; to help women find a way of sharing their ideas about positive ageing so that they have a better quality of life, and so that this phase of their lives is their best. Rather than being something to dread, we should embrace the ageing process.

What next for me? Who knows where life will take me. One thing is for sure: I want to continue being a trailblazer and an inspirational woman. I will always be there to try to improve things for women suffering with the menopause, when they feel low and lost. I will forever continue to lobby for change to combat ageism in all walks of life. For young and old. The youngsters of today will be the old folk of tomorrow. It is vital we have intergenerational discussion to pave the way forward so no one feels voiceless, lost and invisible as they age. We only have one shot at this living lark so we need to sort it out as best we can. I was lost when I was stuck in one place. Now that

I never know where I am going, I am found. I love waking up to extraordinary views and wondering where my life will lead me.

Yes, I have had both good and bad times, particularly during the second coronavirus lockdown. But I wouldn't change anything for the world. I roamed the country on a mission to help women by showing the reality of my life. I think people connect with my story because I have been honest, heartfelt and brave over the last three years. I came out of the wreckage of my life as it was and figured out a way to have what I wanted. But you don't have to make drastic changes and get rid of your home and possessions and take to the road in a motorhome. You can just make simple lifestyle changes to enhance your life and feel happier. At the end of the day that is all we want: to be happy. We do not have to settle for the cards that we are dealt in life as we get older. We may be scared by situations. That fear can actually propel us forward to achieve great things. I tell myself to 'just do it' when I am afraid and somehow things work out. We can create our own destiny and future happiness. Life can be adventurous and positive. For me, personally, it is a great feeling being a retirement rebel, knowing that I have been able to turn my life around, from being broken in my mid-fifties, to feeling the happiest that I have ever been in my life at sixty-three, and feeling fixed.

About the Author

Siobhan Daniels is a retired television and radio journalist who worked for the BBC for thirty years. In 2019, after selling most of her possessions and putting her old life into storage, she hit the road in her new motorhome to begin a retirement less ordinary, travelling the country defying stereotypes and spreading a positive-ageing message. As well as working for the BBC, she has written for or been featured in a variety of magazines and newspapers, including the *Guardian*, *Daily Telegraph* and *Yorkshire Life*, and she gives talks to Women's Institute groups. Siobhan lives wherever she parks her motorhome. Find out more at *shuvonshuvoff.co.uk*